STRIKE THE BULL'S EYE

*Getting God
to Move When You Pray*

AYODEJI AWE

A wholly owned subsidiary of **TBN**

Strike the Bull's Eye: Getting God to Move When You Pray
Trilogy Christian Publishers A Wholly Owned Subsidiary of Trinity Broadcasting Network
2442 Michelle Drive Tustin, CA 92780

Rights Department, 2442 Michelle Drive, Tustin, CA 92780.
Trilogy Christian Publishing/TBN and colophon are trademarks of Trinity Broadcasting Network.
Cover design by: Trilogy
For information about special discounts for bulk purchases, please contact Trilogy Christian Publishing.
Trilogy Disclaimer: The views and content expressed in this book are those of the author and may not necessarily reflect the views and doctrine of Trilogy Christian Publishing or the Trinity Broadcasting Network.
Manufactured in the United States of America
10 9 8 7 6 5 4 3 2 1
Library of Congress Cataloging-in-Publication Data is available.
ISBN: 979-8-89041-069-6
E-ISBN: 979-8-89041-070-2

DEDICATION

This book is dedicated to my precious mother of blessed memory, Mrs. (Deaconess) Elizabeth Omolewa Awe, who powerfully stepped into the role of father and mother after my father unexpectedly passed away at a relatively young age. She single-handedly, by the grace of God, raised the children—five of us—to become ones that will carry on the family legacy of unassailable faith in the Lord and pastoral ministry. I watched her pray her suddenly truncated family into immediately needed supplies that continued till we all broke through. As a woman who knew how to successfully entreat God, she was a treasure for me in the art of prayer, from which I learned and for which I'm most grateful for life.

She was called back home to glory in November 2014. Sweet is the memory of the just.

ACKNOWLEDGMENT

Typing and first editing—Dr. Evelyn Fisher.

Typesetting, beautification, and final arrangement of the script—Olajumoke Awe.

All around and trade-off support—my wife and children.

Prayer support—Our Savior's Church members.

TABLE OF CONTENTS

PREFACE

Imagine a world where you could communicate directly with the creator of the universe—what a privilege that would be! That is the essence of prayer, but let's be honest, it's not always easy. Do you struggle with prayer? Do you feel like your prayers are hitting the ceiling and falling back down? Maybe you are not even sure where to begin.

This book tackles these common prayer issues head-on. It dives deep into the reasons why some people don't pray at all and why others pray but don't seem to get answers. It addresses the time constraints that prevent people from praying, especially those in leadership positions in their churches. But most importantly, it provides practical guidance on how to make prayer work for you.

If you are ready to take your prayer life to the next level and experience a deeper connection with God, then this book is for you. It defines prayer and its purpose and explores the conditions necessary for effective prayer. You will learn how to make your prayers more meaningful and how to develop a regular prayer routine that works for you.

So, whether you are a seasoned prayer warrior or just starting out, this book will equip you with the tools you need to make your prayer life more impactful and fulfilling.

Don't miss out on the opportunity to communicate with the creator of the universe—let's dive in together!

Evelyn O. Fisher
PharmD, RPh
Amazing Grace Pharmacy

PROLOGUE

Nothing is more gratifying than knowing that the million in your very own bank account is securely yours while an ignorant brash fellow that ran to you in a brief gas station encounter disparagingly yelled at you, "Get out my sight, you poor wretched fellow!" All you would do is smile because you know what you know, that you are a rich man by any standard. You are in the bracket that the majority on earth will love to be. You are sure of what you are sure of.

God doesn't lie, neither is He liable to make gaffes. He is deadly serious when He says, "Call unto me, and I will answer you and show you great and mighty things that you do not know." It is forever His pleasure to help and bless us. Scripture contains chronicles of humans like us who proved the veracity of God on this declaration and subject matter. They walked with God and achieved success in prayer. They accomplish so much using prayer as a tool.

But there is a problem today; many of us are frustrated in the place of prayer. We feel futile and unfulfilled. It must be clarified, however, that God has nothing to do with our failure and futility in prayer. It's all our fault at 101 percent.

Nevertheless, *Strike the Bull's Eye* has come for a rescue mission. It presents spiritual insights: truths unveiled and propelled by its spiritual sagacity that will make you a marksman-prayer warrior.

Adopting the title *Strike the Bull's Eye* is intended to convey a message that you can inject 101 percent confidence and swag into your prayer life that when you call on God, He not only hears but listens and, beyond that, responds. I don't know about you; nothing is more frustrating than to be stiffed by the person you are addressing. If you feel that way with man, who you know is limited, to begin with, how much more with God, who you know has all the knowledge, power, and capabilities? Coming to God on any matter is as far as it gets: the end of the road concerning your needs, desire, and destiny. If I end with God, I want Him to answer me. But how practically sad that oftentimes, we are frustrated because not much is accomplished when we come to God in prayer.

This book intends to show you how to change that completely. There is a new path created that will give you confidence that God hears and will answer when you pray. It's like a marksman shooting the bull straight in the eye. That's not a feat for a novice. Many with a gun can get their prey in any part of the body, but it takes a highly trained, skilled hunter to shoot the bull at its very eye. It's the precision of the marksman that separates him from the vast ordinary.

This book will train you to be a sharpshooter in the altar of grace and mercy so that not only will you be confident to approach God, but often you will joyfully testify of the goodness of the Lord with more to show in your life for your prayer. God is like a vast, inexhaustible ocean; in prayer, you can get as much as you want from Him. The better part of the story is that He is willing to be tapped.

Precisely striking a bull in the eye is not a feat for a novice. Such is reserved only for skilled sharpshooters. That is the miracle this book will perform in your life, that when you pray, God cannot but answer. That is a giant stride that puts you in a special class reserved for those who have mastered the art of praying and had and will continue to enjoy the needed interventions and the resultant abundance that God had reserved for His children.

You are set to become a prayer geek who, like a marksman hitting the bull's eye with impunity, would pray in a manner that God cannot ignore you. On that platform, God moves on your behalf whenever you pray. This book is leading you into a new season of life. As you respond appropriately, enjoy the new status and season. Let's go!

INTRODUCTION

In the area of prayers, there are many different issues that could confront a man.

There are many whose problems have to do with not praying. These kinds of people can't just pray. They won't pray. Either due to lack of guts, intuition, or time, it is futile to want to know the reason; the end result is that no prayers are said. Therefore, there is a void in their lives created by lack due to no allocation through the provisional grace of prayer.

Yet, there are those who could pray and do pray. Their issue is never the lack of prayer but commensurate answer to the volume of prayers. In this compartment, there is little blessing and divine intervention to show for a sweat-soaked basketful of prayers. At the end of the day, the result is the same as those who cannot or do not pray.

May be there are those who pray too little or not enough. Sometimes, surprisingly are found in this group those that are not expected to belong. Dennis Rainer, in his book *The Post-Quarantine Church*, confessed to be one.[1] He is a big shot in the church. In his interaction with some pastors, he discovered that he was not alone in this predicament. It wasn't the case of not being dutiful as pastors and leaders in the church; it was that some other more compelling pastoral duties have a way of pushing prayers to the secondary tier.

For this high-profile group, it would seem like many found it easier to talk about it or call or teach others to pray than actually pray. Easier said than done is the parable here. If there is such a challenge at the pulpit, imagine the severity at the pews! How dire is the problem in this arena? There would be no distinctive instrument to properly gauge what would or would not have been.

One thing is very clear, though; there are things: knowledge to have, information on hand, situation on the ground, and conditions to be met in order for prayers to be "money." In the productive equation of prayer, the right variables must be in the right and blended proportions. At the end of the day, it is what heavens graciously release to the earth that defines the effectiveness or efficacy of the prayers of the righteous to the holy and gracious God, who is ready and willing to do good to His children; all things being equal.

This book is set to provide much of what a believer can be opened to, to transport him into a plat where his prayers will begin to be fruitful and results compiling.

Remember that God is always willing to hear the prayers of the righteous; as a matter of fact, His ears are set close to ours, and His eyes are set upon ours (Luke chapter 11, 1 Peter 3:12).

CHAPTER 1:
WHAT IS PRAYER

A humble heart doesn't kick against the conclusion that in all realms and in all things, man ought to defer to God. That is prayer! Man, totally deferring to God.

Prayer is calling unto God. When we call upon the Lord, we are seeking His attention. Prayer demands God to look at me. Though there might be several other places that demand His attention, at my prayer mode, I'm saying God, regardless, look at my side. Thank the same God; His eyes are not restricted; they can go to and from the earth instantaneously to reveal His power to intervene in as many situations and at the same time (2 Chronicles 16:9). This puts a prayer person in no disadvantage of any sort.

So, prayer is calling upon the Lord (either verbally or nonverbally, according to Victor Ehiemua),[2] the One who is worthy to be called by His personality and definition at any time when help is needed. He is God, our Creator, the Designer of all that we see as we are today. Creation was His thoughtful design and at His own will and violation.

And to the best of His ability and the evidenced result, as we see it, He did a great job.

You and I are beautifully, fearfully, and meticulously made and, in His exquisite image, endowed personally with all the tangibles and the intangibles—from being a creature with purpose and intelligence to men who are fully provided for as we live our lives. Let me remind you that He provided resources bountifully for five and half days before He made man so that from the moment man steps on the cosmos, with his livelihood and intelligence, he would lack nothing. In our limitation, if there be any, and no sooner than we saw that there are, giving us the confidence of His good intent at creating us, He gave us a blank check: "Call unto me, and I will answer thee, and show thee great and mighty things, which thou knowest not" (Jeremiah 33:3, KJV).

The psalmist reminds us that "God is our refuge and strength, a very present help in trouble" (Psalm 46:1, KJV), not only in time of trouble but at all times. Following all these brings a man to a comfortable platform of praying, which means that whenever we feel we are faced with a duty or anything for that matter that is bigger or too profound for us to deal with, we already have the approval of calling on God for help. Therefore, we say that prayer is demanding God's attention for the purpose of helping us.

Prayer is closeness to God. By demanding help from someone, no matter either by physical closeness or proxy, if help is obtained, there will be closeness. That man is able to call upon the Lord, and He is able to hear him has in itself established the fact of closeness. In the era of scientific breakthrough, this concept should not be too difficult to grasp. Even as man to man, we pick up our phone and dial another at the far end of the earth, and we speak to each other. Electronically, we mail information and exchange pleasantries. Through satellites, pictures and images of real-life situations are delivered to small and great distances. All these human ways of calling on one another or connecting validate the ease at which a man can call upon the Lord, underscoring the closeness factor.

Closeness, as a definition of prayer, credentials the effectiveness of proximity of the One who is unlimited— the "factory" of life and all of its accessories, implying that at all times, man is covered when God is near. No wonder Moses prayed as the Lord's orchestrated deliverance journey of his people was about to commence—"If your Presence does not go with us, do not send us up from here" (Exodus 33:15, NIV). Confidence to proceed in life is surely hinged on God's proximity, and a smart one at that. Therefore, when you are close to God, you are in prayer, meaning that help is readily available. Now I can understand the mindset of Sadhu Sundar Singh:

> *The essence of prayer does not consist in asking God for something but in opening our hearts to God, in speaking with Him, and living with Him in perpetual communion.*

Prayer is continual abandonment to God. Prayer does not mean asking God for all kinds of things we want; it is rather the desire for God Himself, the only Giver of life. Prayer is not asking but union with God. Prayer is not painful effort to gain from God's help in the varying needs of our lives. Prayer is the desire to possess God Himself, the Source of all life. The true spirit of prayer does not consist in asking for blessings but in receiving Him, who is the Giver of all blessings, and in living a life of fellowship with Him.[3]

Closeness to God can be achieved when you open your heart (i.e., you are willing) to the God who is yearning to come in any way. You may also get this done by creating a space in the physical, telling God your desire to have Him with you exclusively. Andrew Murray confidently recommends this to be our chief object in prayer, instructing us to shut the world out, withdraw from all worldly thoughts and occupation, and lock ourselves in alone with God, to pray to or be with Him in secret.[4] To him, one-on-one with God without any other is an effective prayer.

No one can be faulted in referring to this phenomenon as securing God Himself. That is a huge accomplishment by all standards. When God, the Creator, all-knowing, all-powerful, and all-present, is in the books, you are successful in prayer.

Prayer is the expression of our dependency on God.

Sometimes, asking for a help from another human or any place may not necessarily define our dependency, but when seeking for help is directed at God, the moralized definition kicks in that our dependency is on Him. The psalmist demonstrated this very tacitly when he proclaimed: "I will lift up mine eyes unto the hills [i.e., God is regarded living at the higher enclave], from whence cometh my help. My help cometh from the LORD [the chief master], which made heaven and earth [exclusively, Darwin is a joker!]¹ (Psalm 121:1–2, KJV). God is in His own exclusive club, confident and unassuming. Conversely presenting the invincibility of His prowess as the One who can take care of whatever need may face a human, He declares: "Their sorrows shall be multiplied that hasten after another god" (Psalm 16:4a, KJV). In Isaiah 32:33, He weighed in on His people's foolishness at sidelining His help by seeking help from the Assyrians. He castigated them for it. He pointedly revealed how economically deranged such a move was, that racked in such a staggering cost with nothing creditworthy to ultimately show for it. He furthermore moved to expose the frailty and limitedness of the wrong helper by stripping them of their security.

A man whose heart and mouth convince the Lord that He is his all in all is a man of prayer because God never puts to shame those who trust in and depend totally on Him. His muscles flex when the signal of our dependency is successfully transmitted to Him. Let's make progress to

---

1 Hereinafter, brackets added for clarity.

size up prayer in a more engaging way:

PRAYER IS A BATTLEFIELD

Prayers are necessitated when there are situations that need to be bettered. Sometimes, these situations could be war-zonal in nature. In such cases, the battles must be fought in the place of prayer. John H. Jowett sees things in this light when he strongly observes that *prayer is a battlefield where life's critical battles are won or lost.*[5] Therefore in prayer, we fight when the cause demands it. Paul shared with us that he fought some beasts at Ephesus. He wasn't referring to goats or leopards; these are enemies in the realm of the unseen. In one of his epistles, the word of the Lord teaches us that we do not fight against flesh and blood but against principalities, powers, the rulers of darkness of this world, and spiritual wickedness in high places (Ephesians 6:12). Therefore, he charged us to put on the whole armor of God that we may be able to stand against the wiles of the devil (verse 11).

Being confronted with issues that are hardly physical or that originate from the unseen, though may show up in the visible, however, requires prayer as the only possible effective weapon. In the scripture, we have found of a time when the Lord Himself struck people with incurable diseases as was with Jehoram, son of Jehoshaphat (2 Chronicles 21:15–17). Incurable in the sense that with the best human effort, there can be no relief; only the Lord (Invisible) who called it in can deal with it.

In Isaiah chapter 38 and 2 Kings chapter 20, the Lord determined that Hezekiah's work on earth was to be terminated and struck him with boil. Efforts to get it healed proved abortive until he cried to God and reminded Him of usefulness of his life and the good seeds of life that he had sowed into God. He probably reminded the Lord of His word that the righteous and their labors of love carried out in the name of the Lord will be rewarded (Proverbs 11:30, 1 Corinthians 15:58). Then was God appeased. He thereafter sent Prophet Isaiah to intervene and revert the impending doom (Isaiah chapter 38).

Worse still is when the devil and/or his cortege are the aggressors. We are warned, albeit very sternly, that though we are in the flesh, the wars we face cannot be fought physically. For the weapon of warfare are not carnal (physical) but are mighty through God to the pulling down of strongholds, casting down imaginations and every high thing that exalts itself against the knowledge of God, and bringing into captivity every thought to the obedience of Christ (2 Corinthians 10:3–5).

In other words, such attacks are strongholds. They come opposing as indescribable potent forces, and the only way and weapon ordained to deal with them is spiritual. We are reminded that we cannot fight the spirit with our fists or guns. It takes prayers, i.e., God's intervention, to route spiritual forces. For we overcome by the blood of the Lamb and the word of our own testimony (Revelation 12:11). We are given a name that is highly exalted above every other name that at the name of Jesus, every knee should bow of things in heaven and things in earth and things under the earth (Philippians 2:10). The name of the Lord is an attacking machine against any formation against us. It is far superior. No wonder we are confided—no weapon formed against us can prosper and that in all these things, we are more than conquerors through Christ that loves us (Isaiah 57:17, Romans 8:37).

Prayer is also our defense system. There are times when the enemy attacks, when we only need to be defended and saved. The Lord, in these circumstances, reminds us that the name of the Lord is a mighty tower, the righteous run into it and are safe (Proverbs 18:10).

PRAYER IS A MINISTRY

As a ministry, the manifestation of the spirit of God occurs as men and women are recruited into the vocation of praying and interceding.

Because of the ongoing activities of Satan and his followers in the evil-infested world (also caused by Satan), God has felt the need to neutralize this omen by raising a ministry of prayer.

Following severally, we are admonished to pray. God's people are enjoined to pray without ceasing (1 Thessalonians 5:17). Pray for one another, our leaders, the government, the apostles, and missionaries Paul charged (1 Thessalonians 5:25, 2 Thessalonians 3:1, Hebrews 13:18).

It is evident that there has to be a sustained level of prayer activities to downplay the satanic throes and minimize his tentacles, especially for the sake of the righteous and the church. Therefore, apart from the individual need-urged prayers, some are conscripted into active prayer life propped by the power of the Holy Spirit. They operate in the intercessory mode and offer prayers that create powerful forces that must overtake, overturn, and demolish the evil agendas and activities of Satan and his lieutenants in this world.

For instance, early in the New Testament church, James was arrested for preaching the gospel and was killed. The foes of the new church, seeing that no one raised an objection, came back to arrest Peter with the aim of killing him, like they did James. But following Peter's arrest, the Holy Spirit went into action in the church and moved them to begin intercession. They universally went into prayers that were mandated to split the intent of the church's enemy. Thanks to God, He heard their prayers and rolled into action. Result: Peter was released, and the church phased into another round of development and growth.

PRAYER IS A CREATOR OF FORCES OF CHANGE

Prayer is a change creator. Whenever prayers come into a place, certain forces are created that influence that environment. God is a creator, and whenever He shows up, things change. There is power in the name of Jesus.

Whenever that name is called, things begin to change. Surely there is power in the name of the Lord.

At the mention of the name of Jesus, every kneel begins to bow, and every tongue confesses that He is Lord. The establishment of the name of Jesus creates an unmatchable force that sends packing everything that attempts to exalt itself above God. That was what their master, the devil, the archenemy of God, stood for. The name of Jesus, as in prayer, has been given as a greater force to discomfit every other power and attempt to dent our peace.

The forces created in prayer change from bad to good, good to better, and better to best for all and things on the side of God. But for any anti-god activities, things must turn for the worse for them. There is no peace for the wicked because they will not go unpunished, says the Lord.

CHAPTER 2:

ESSENTIALITY OF PRAYER

The patent of man and his bright future, undercut by his frailty, his limitedness, and satanic wiles, have left him with no wiser alternative than to relish in the relying on God, which, indeed, is the definition of prayer.

Why is prayer necessary in the life of a believer? What calls for it? Why do we need to pray? Why, in fact, do we pray? Why can't I do without it? These are some questions that will be answered in the exposition of this chapter.

We do know that the world at creation was good and excellently created. God the Creator Himself attested to the excellence in creation. "God saw all that he had made, and it was very good" (Genesis 1:31a, NIV). "The heavens declare the glory of God; the skies proclaim the work of his hands" (Psalm 19:1, NIV).

However, the interruption of the beauty of the earth

came following the insurrection of Lucifer, son of the morning. Satan, who used to be the commander of the supreme of God's angels, suddenly became high-minded and sought to elevate himself above God, his Creator (Isaiah 14:12). Following this brazen act, he, with about one-third of the angelic hosts (who supported his revolt), was expelled from heaven and thrust into the earth. Perhaps humans would probably have never known how calamitous his imposed entry into earth would be for men had the hosts of heaven not expressed pity for the sons of men: "[...] Woe to the inhabiters of the earth and of the sea! for the devil is come down unto you, having great wrath, because he knoweth that he hath but a short time" (Revelation 12:12b, KJV).

Invariably as it would practically turn out, the world became a very complex place soonest Satan and all his stooges entered. And, of course, the scripture enlightens us as to why this had to be. Now we have come to understand that Satan's threefold ministry is deadly—he operates to kill, steal, and destroy. His main targets are those related to God. He visits his animosity for God upon those who are named with Him. His animated vengefulness toward God has rendered him the dubious designation of "Chief adversary" (1 Peter 5:8); therefore, a very big need for prayer. Martin Luther, the grandfather of Reformation, spoke of the reality and relevance mindset when he observed: "If I fail to spend two hours in prayer each morning, the devil gets the victory through the day. I have so much business I cannot get on without spending three hours daily in prayer."[6]

Considering the enormity and graveness of his operation, a believer cannot but seek God's help and power to stay immovable or repel his attack. Somehow, we realize quickly that we stand no other recourse than to go to God in prayer. I so much believe Victor Ehiemua was thinking alongside me when he expressed that praying is not an option but a necessity as the air we breathe. He further urged his readers to pray, pray, and keep praying.[7]

Though the earth has been yielded to man to have dominion over, however, because the angels are ranked higher in power at creations (remember that Satan is an archangel himself), they had easily hijacked the authority over the operations of this earth (Psalm 8:5). Thus, he earned the reputation "god of this world." He is the master of the universe. He is capable of walking to and fro the length and breadth of the earth doing what he does best—the ministry of wreaking havoc in contrast to Christ who is anointed to do good works (Luke 4:18). Satan's threefold ministry— "steal, and to kill, and to destroy" (John 10:10a, KJV) is a back scratcher that requires any sane man to develop a longer hand capable of nursing a wound when it is sustained down the lower back. No more effective methodology. Also, because of the unrestricted power and freedom of Satan, he evangelizes and then recruits followers. Since the followers and his stooges will carry out the schemes of their leader, Satan, evil and sin have come to geometrically multiply (Matthew 24:14). Therefore, because of this spread of evil,

Christ Himself warns us to be aware and takes steps ahead of the cunning acts of Satan—the days are definitely evil.

Following carefully the advice of the one who died for us, we must come to grasp that to live a purposeful and achieving life, man must be prayerful always, for that matter (Luke 18:1).

Again, bear in mind that when we pray, we are seeking God's help in a bid to advance. Satan stands for the opposition. He desires to stop a child of God from advancing to achieve his purpose by first attempting to kill. If he cannot achieve killing, which, in most cases, has to get God's approval, he would resort to stealing good things and blessings that rightly belong to us. If and when he fails in doing that, he will seek to destroy our valuables.

How does he achieve any or all of this? He capitalizes on our weaknesses on one hand and on the other, our rebellion against God. When God's hands are lifted off us due to our miscues and sins, then he is able to come in and meddle with us (Job chapter 1).

But thank God that in spite of the huge power of Satan on earth, the One who has the possession of all the power is still on our side. All power on earth and heaven has been given to Christ, and if we belong to Him and walk with Him in a prayerful manner, we are able to do all things because He will strengthen us (Matthew 28:20, Philippians 4:13). With our limitedness, it is very critical to seek the unlimitedness of God in balancing the forces of Satan upon this earth to which we are all susceptible since we are still living in this world. This is a very pivotal reason why we need prayers, that is, constantly calling upon the Lord for help. It is highly fitting the way Corrie ten Boom expresses her thoughts on this matter: "Don't pray when you feel like it. Have an appointment with the Lord and keep it. A man is powerful on his knees."[8] With the tentacles of Satan and his lieutenants widely spread, a man needs a time with God early in the morning before commencing the activities of the day, in the first month of the year to begin the journey of the year, and at eve before sleep, which gets one into and safely through the arena of the pestilences that stalk by night (Psalm 91:6, NIV).

John Bunyan, the famed writer of one of the greatest classics of faith, *Pilgrim's Progress*, had this to say regarding the must-have prayer with God at the critical times of the day and night. "He who runs from God in the morning will scarcely find Him the rest of the day."[9] You ask, "And so what?" The bitter fact is, there are some people you don't have to have in your life to succeed, but very certainly, there are specific people that must be on your side for your life to not be short-circuited and for you to succeed. In this respect, God occupies a very unique, distinctive position. That is why I agree with Bunyan; if God has to be with me to make my day, I'd better engage Him early so that I can be maximized. Moreover, he likes those who seek Him early; He readily makes Himself and His grace available to such (Psalm 63:1–8; 119:2–3). Having the Lord with us, as Moses demanded, is a smart thing to do; it is a must for the wise. This is achieved through prayer.

If prayer is this vital and essential for any man, more so, it would be on a larger scale for a minister. I mean those who stand day and night to impart our lives with the divine touches of God. Wisdom has alerted us that when you represent God in any capacity, you run a certain high-profile risk with the archenemy. Because you are identified with Christ in service, Satan runs after you, not necessarily because of you but more so because of what you stand for. His greatest goal is to have the work of God derailed, and so he would go at length to bring you down or take you out, whichever comes readily handy. It is the more reason why a minister must be armed with prayer, either by himself or, in addition, by intercession of others. Apostle Peter puts us on alert! "Be sober, be vigilant; because your adversary the devil, as a roaring lion, walketh about seeking whom he may devour: Whom resist steadfast in faith, knowing that the same afflictions are accomplished in your brethren that are in the world. But the God of all grace…" (1 Peter 5:8–10a, KJV) Edward Payson got the message when he professed: "Prayer is the first thing, the second thing, the third thing necessary to a minister. Pray, then, my dear brothers, 'Pray, pray, and pray.'"[10] He reminds me of Apostle Paul writing to the Thessalonians, "Pray without ceasing" (1 Thessalonians 5:17, KJV). Hear, E. M. Bounds echoes similar thoughts:

The men who have done the most for God in this world have been early on their knees. He who fritters away the early morning, its opportunity and freshness, in other pursuits than seeking God will make poor headway seeking Him the rest of the day. If God is not first in our thoughts and efforts in the morning, He will be in the last place the remainder of the day.[11]

Beloved, the old gospel song my parents used to sing in church reminds us of the essentiality of prayer: "Prayer is the key, prayer is the key, prayer is the master key; Jesus started with prayers and ended with prayers; prayer is the master key!"[12]

Bishop Desmond Tutu was once asked about prayer: "Why do you pray?" Phillip Yancey, in his book titled *Prayer: Does It Make Any Difference*, quoted his answer that is very fitting here:

If your day starts off wrong, it stays skewed. What I have found is that getting up a little earlier and trying to have an hour of quiet in the presence of God, mulling over some scripture, supports me. I try to have a map in my mind of the world and I go around the world, continent by continent—only Africa I try to do in a little more detail—and offer all of that to God.[13]

PRAYING (TO GOD) IS A PREFERRED METHOD OF SEEKING HELP

Praying to God for help is a choice amongst other possibilities but with a higher degree of certainty and help. We do know that sometimes there are alternative sources of help that may be sought by humans, but wisdom dictates that not all sources have same capabilities and outcomes. For instance, man can seek financial help from man, the devil, or God. For sure, if you are not related to a person, he would give you conditions for his help, especially if you are not looking for just pennies. You will need to tread gently and carefully so you won't get him upset to the point of changing his mind and backing out of his promised help. Banks would give you statutory conditions and restrictions if you secured such help.

Turning to Satan definitely takes you into a twist. He is a focused daredevil with his uttermost goals uncompromised. He deals with man shrewdly with the end in close view—to kill, steal, and destroy. You want help? He readily will oblige but with a costly string attached. Many who have sought that kind of help he had helped by using one of his most powerful agents: Mammon. He "blesses" but conscripts one to pick up a bag of sorrow as an attachment. That is why Jesus our Lord hints us that it is extremely hard for a rich man to experience eternal bliss: "It would be easier for a camel to pass through the eye of a needle than for a rich man to enter heaven" (Matthew

19:24, KJV) (paraphrased). The rich he is referring to are the ones "blessed" by the master controller of the universe, the prince of the earth: the devil. Yes, he is a helper. Yet he is in a severe class of his own. Yes, he will "supply," but he will knock your head. Love is not found in the dictionary of Satan. He is the wicked one. He helps in order to kill. That is the depth of the psalmist's encouragement for believers who are not patient to be blessed of God but daily get exasperated by the wealth of the ungodly. David is cautious and exhorts: Be not envious of the wicked when they prosper; it is because they will be cut down and will shortly perish. He goes further, but trust in the Lord, and you shall inherit the land (Psalm 37:9–11). God's help establishes not only for the present but more for the future. Its longevity is enticing; the more reason why prayer is a needful practice of life.

This goes on to buttress the point in this subtopic that the help of God is superior and more certain and lastingly peaceful and blessed: a very special respite when compared with every other source. He blesses without adding sorrow (Proverbs 10:22). That is why praying to Him is a wise thing to do. Great saints of old, like David, discovered this wisdom in their time, and no wonder in their chronicles, we read so much of breakthroughs and victories (Psalm 118:6–29 passim).

Praying to the Lord for a help or a need to be met is in a special class of its own; only the fool will sideline such an opportunity. That is why prayer has assumed a high-profile necessity status for anyone who wants to make the best of life because, as the Father/Creator who knows the end from the beginning, He comes in to assist in consonance with His eternal plans. And because He is unlimited, in comparison with every other source, and can accommodate as much as comes to Him, He would always be preferred by sane minds.

In one of his writing for technology, David Teather mentioned Steve Ballmer, Microsoft CEO, revealing that Bill Gates receives about 4,000 emails per day, though most of it is spam.[14] This was in 2004. It was more than any human could handle. I believe he reacted appropriately to this enormous surge to arm his computer with software that filters through his emails, allowing only important messages through and sending other letters to electronic oblivion. Bill Gates, though intelligent and revolvingly one of the top two or three richest on earth in our time, is a mortal being; he is human. There is a limit to him and what he can do, no matter how much he loves and desires to do. He cannot respond to all nor attempt to answer all of their computer queries.

This story emblemizes man, you and I included. Man is limited as a source of help. The devil is a man-spirit. He has powers, but his mission renders his power dangerous and his help dubious. To dine with him as a source of help, as some sage suggested, you must procure a long spoon. And to him, as a source of help, you must count your cost ahead of time, and the cost could be very high. I bet that it will outweigh the benefit. No supply or help of Satan is worth your soul. Jesus forewarned: what shall it profit a man if he gains the whole world and loses his soul, or what shall a man give in exchange for his soul! We are reminded that their sorrows shall be multiplied, that hasten after another god (other than the true God) (Psalm 16:4).

But God is the good God, our defender, a very present help, omnipresent, omniscient, and omnipotent. God, in contrast to man and the devil, has unlimited capacity to help. Bishop Wale Oke describes Him as an ocean, way vast and big; nothing moves Him. You get out of Him as much as you believe when you seek Him and His face.[15] Usually, this is through the mechanism called prayer.

That is why prayer is of uttermost importance. You must pray because nothing else is more effective as a source of help, and He demands that you call upon Him for help whenever you need to. He is not tired of listening to us, nor is He irritated by the frequency of demand for His attention. He is a willing and always available consultant of dealing with the complex issues. That makes perfect sense because nothing is better than relying on the One who started it all—the Creator Himself, God. Though He yielded the earth to a tussle between man and Satan, we know that man would have an upper hand if he held on to the apron of God. Though the angels (Satan included) were created superior in personal power, however in Christ, a believer can access a higher and greater power to dislodge Satan. This can only be done through prayer. That was the big emphasis in the declaration of Martin Luther: "If I fail to spend a certain time in prayer, the devil gets the victory."[16]

In the realm of the Spirit, Jesus exposed a tactic often used by the enemy to deal with the Body of Christ on earth. "Smite the shepherd, and the sheep shall be scattered" (Zechariah 13:7, KJV), dropped Jesus, warning that the ministers, pastors, apostles, and church leaders need to be extra protected because the enemy would deal blows on the body by taking the head. Again, it boils down to prayer as the defense mechanism.

Satan used this ploy in the early church resulting in James being arrested and put to death. Seeing that no big noise or protest was made, he proceeded to arrest Peter and proposed taking him out too. But thanks to the Lord, the spirit of God jolted the church into standing up against the enemy's wiles by coming together united in prayer and intercession for Peter. Result: Heaven responded and sent a rescue operation. Prayer quelled the cruel tactic of the enemy (Acts 12:1–19).

CHAPTER 3:

FACILITATORS OF PRAYERS

Certain foods are not meant to be eaten by man uncooked or unsalted. In this regard, high degree heat and salt are essential condiments that must be admitted to a pleasurable table of humans, not animals. So, it is with prayer venture. There are conditions upon which our trip to the altar of prayer is approved and regarded, without which our petitions become mere utterances.

The facilitators of prayers can be defined as the key ingredients that form a prayer. They are those items that must be on the ground for the building of prayer to be erected. They are the foundations, formatting the strength of prayer definition—the power and effectiveness, potency factor, without which prayer cannot be prayer but mere words which cannot for one moment steal the attention of God. When the facilitators are available, prayer could then be offered. Some of those facilitators of prayer include:

1. FAITH

Faith is the cord that ties a great relationship. It is a flow of connectivity between two people who are in a deep relationship. It depicts a form of waves that is in a perpetual linkage with people or entities whose hearts are open to each other.

It could be defined as a trust factor. In the scriptures, faith is defined as the substance of things hoped for, evidence of things not yet seen (Hebrews 11:1). Faith presupposes that something is going to happen assuredly; though it is not in sight yet, however, the confirmation is real. The scripture tenders that the fathers of faith and many who related to God before our time were highly regarded for having faith in God that some things He promised them or things they believed Him for would happen. We are told they obtained excellent reports because eventuality proved their faith right and genuine.

Put in a very simple format, prayer cannot be called a prayer if the one offering it does not believe that God will do what one is asking. In other words, for any to pray and be effective, he has to have the faith that God will answer. That faith encompasses the fact that He hears us when we call Him and that He is able to answer and is willing to consent. No wonder the writer of Hebrews in the popular section that eulogized faith declares, "But without faith it is impossible to please Him, for he who comes to God [in prayers] must believe that He is, and that He is a rewarder of those who diligently seek Him" (Hebrews 11:6, NKJV).

Faith is further defined by the quantum of the belief input. Belief thrives on the notable character of God that He is good and is willing to take care of the faithful—those who are related to Him. He is the God who takes care of business regardless of what. He is very committed to the terms of the relationship between Him and His people.

Scripture gave us a full dose of God's recorded dealing with His people, those in relationship with Him when need arose and how God responded valiantly and precisely. God has been found trustworthy and reliable. He is a great protector and mighty defender.

Reading through scripture and knowing these awesome facts about God is faith-building. Faith, when built, motivates us to pray. Knowing that God is a prayer answering God gives us the boldness and confidence to call on Him whenever we feel like we need help.

Here in present is the power of testimonies in our worship services today. When people testify of what God is doing in their lives, many who have the feelings that God no longer intervenes in people's daily lives begin to resuscitate from their mundane indolent mindset.

There are many today who think that since the Bible days, graphic divine interventions no longer occur. Some of these people though may be Christians, their lifestyles or what their pastors (especially some in the non-Pentecostal circles) teach them have deserted the belief that prayer is still a vibrant instrument that brings God into our situation. Therefore, to people like this, faith is a stranger, and prayer is just an academic practice known but rarely practiced, and even for some when practiced, it is just a routine action—no tangible result is expected. In this mode, faith is near nonexistent and pathetically inactive, while prayer is atypical.

Knowing about God, His capabilities, His goodness, love, and willingness to help, and the fact that He will do what is good for His children, partly automatically and partly due to our prayers, is a powerful ingredient of faith. When this is in operation as a basis to our prayer, such a prayer becomes effective because God answers. Faith moves the hands of God concerning our situations handled with prayer. Remember again that without faith, it is impossible to please God. Those who will come to God (for anything) must believe that He is available and that He responds to the call of those who approach Him (Hebrews 11:6).

Personally, my prayer life is built upon two strong factors among others. I opened my eyes to this life in the hands of parents who love to pray. My father and mother (pastor and wife) loved to pray. They were both raised by the spiritually strong man of God, the founder of Christ Apostolic Church, Apostle Joseph Ayo Babalola. (He needs no further introduction from those who are conversant with Christian churches in Nigeria and Africa). Secondly,

I lost my father when I was eight. With his death, lost for me were a lot of privileges. My mother was a very tough woman in every area of life, prayer inclusive. However, two hands sometimes cannot perform as efficiently as four steady hands, especially in the area of provisions. This has actually pushed me into prayers earlier in life than many of my age group, perhaps.

I saw my mom pray hard; I did the same. But then, in my own confines, I had some needs across the spectra of life landscape that my mother could not easily come through for me. I personally decided to offer a helping hand to her and myself by stepping up in prayer. And boy, God has pleasure in answering young people's prayers—I am a living witness, and I give glory to God. I don't know fully why, but it may be because not many young people do, and the few who do touch the tender, merciful heart of God. I do know later, eventually, that God loves young people to be dependent upon Him. I believe He uses this as a symbol of the required state of mind of all who will enjoy God's fellowships now and in eternity. See how Jesus puts it: "Suffer [allow] the little children to come unto me, and forbid them not: for of such is the kingdom of God" (Mark 10:14b, KJV).

As a young boy with no full parental supply, I ended up having the bests of provision (by His grace)—best school, education, attitude and behavior, provisions, and eventually immigration to the United States, etc. God was good to me as I called upon Him for help. The interesting and motivating part was that the more I saw Him move on my behalf, the more my faith developed, and the more I relied on Him for the care of my needs, provision coming from every direction—my mother and others, etc. This confidence grew to the point that I knew that if I call upon the Lord, any time of the day or night, He will respond.

As I grew older, I began to experience God through a faith that has sprouted in a wider dimension. "What do you mean?" you asked. I began to discover that some requests were not granted either in the form I asked or in a time I demanded. At first, I cautioned to decipher what was going wrong. Was it me, my sin, inadequate prayer, etc.? Was it God? Tired of me, or rejected me? But gradually, the spirit of God began to instruct me that the dimension I was experiencing was a greater level of faith formation whereby you trust God even when your bidding is not released. I was made to understand that anyone that God loves will enjoy His guidance in all spectra of life as He will not retract from giving us the best. Therefore, there are times the answer to our prayer is the non-granting of it, either in content or time. This being because God has a better thing for the same or another time, or He has the same thing for another but better time.

God continued to teach me the importance of maximizing life through the accuracy of answered prayers. His spirit began to teach me that overall, God's plan for His child is beautifully unique and that individually walking with Him obediently and prayerfully makes the implementation easier and better. So, I learned that though a certain prayer may not be "answered" per se, yet it was answered. This learning increased my faith the more, knowing that granted or not, when I have put a request before the Lord, I trust fully that He'll take care of it.

Faith, as an ingredient of prayer, is so important. Hear what Jesus says about it: "If you have faith as small as a mustard seed, you can say to this mulberry tree, 'Be uprooted and planted in the sea,' and it will obey you" (Luke 17:6, NIV). That in itself is very hilarious. How big can a mustard seed be? I tell you, it is really as small as the meaning of the word "small." Therefore, in essence, Jesus is teaching us that a faith of any dimension will generate productivity for our prayers. Most assuredly, believing that God will answer us when we call on Him is a key to entering into the arena of answered prayers.

And indeed, God emphatically demands that from us. "Have faith in God" (Mark 11:22, KJV), Jesus admonished. Meaning: be in the mode whereby you can access things of value from your God. The faithfulness, goodness, large-heartedness, and His love for us are huge credentials that a wise believer should behold, that motivate a spring of faith in the Father God. This was highlighted with a comparison that Christ used in the illustration of this point to his hearers: "Which of you fathers, if your son asks for a fish, will give him a snake instead?" (Luke 11:11, NIV) Yes, the overwhelming consensus is that not many fathers in this world would do that. Men are noted to want to give to and over-pamper their children. So, Jesus' exposition continued the thought, "If you then, being evil, know how to give good gifts to your children, how much more will your heavenly Father give the Holy Spirit to those who ask Him!" (Luke 11:13, NKJV)

To be one who benefits maximally from or through prayer, we must grasp the fact that God, in fact, loves to answer us whenever we call on Him. He never feels disturbed like I do once in a while when my kids come to me at a (human) inconvenient time. With our God, there is no "inconvenience." At all times, He is available; in every place, God is around the corner.

Even with the competition that the magnitude of our problem may present to us sometime, we must endeavor, in the words of Oswald Chambers: "Pray with our eyes on God, not on the difficulties."[17] That in itself quantifies the quality of our faith, which is armed with the appeal to have our prayers favorably answered.

2. RIGHTEOUSNESS

Righteousness is a charter of the relationship between a believer and God that he has put his faith in. The righteous, in the eyes of God, are those who have met His requirements of righteousness. To God, righteousness is attained when the precious blood of Jesus, the beloved Son of God, given as a ransom to die a violent death in exchange for the punishment that the sinner deserves, is applied to the sinful status of any man. The application of the precious blood is evoked by subscribing to the belief of who Jesus is: the Savior of man, for which purpose He died in His place. The subscription is plainly expressed thus: if thou shall believe on the Lord Jesus Christ, thou shall be saved. "If you confess with your mouth the Lord Jesus and believe in your heart that God has raised Him from the dead, you will be saved" (Romans 10:9, NKJV).

The scripture elucidated further—"For God so loved the world, that he gave his only begotten Son, that whosoever believeth in him should not perish, but have everlasting life" (John 3:16, KJV).

Therefore, any who believes in the Lord Jesus in totality and who confesses with his mouth that He was raised from the dead is a righteous man in the sight of God.

One huge benefit accruing from this new status is that the righteous, through his confessed belief, earned the right to call upon the Lord and be heard and replied to. It comes with the package. "But as many as received him, to them gave he power to become the sons of God..." (John 1:12a, KJV) That power extends as far as getting the attention of the Father 24/7. To solidify the point, the word of the Lord tells us, in contrast, that the prayer of the unrighteous is an abomination to the Lord (Proverbs 15:8). Apostle Peter's input on the matter reveals that the eyes of the Lord are over the righteous and His ears are open unto their prayers but the face of the Lord is against those who do evil (1

Peter 3:12).

In Luke chapter 1, when the angel of the Lord visited Zacharias the priest to announce the birth of John the Baptist, he was told that as a righteous man, the Lord had heard his prayers and had decided to answer at this time. Both Zacharias and his wife, Elizabeth, were said to be "righteous before God." No wonder the angel was sent to intimate them of the Lord having heard their prayers.

Being born again is another terminology that is a substitute (John 3:3). All these imply that when one has a valid sonship/daughtership relationship with God, which can only come through belief in Christ Jesus (in this dispensation), then he has punched the ticket to have his prayers heard and attended to by God. Just as a father cannot ignore the call of his child, so God cannot ignore the prayers of the righteous. No wonder, we are told, the righteous cried, and the Lord heard and delivered them out of all of their troubles (Psalm 34:17).

3. PRAISE AND WORSHIP

Praise and worship are the art of prolific powering of praise and worship to God through the mode of words and or singing. It is sometimes accompanied with music— musical instruments playing melody to sweeten the offered words or songs. Praise and worship elevate the spirit and the emotions of both the giver and the receiver. More importantly, it aligns our spirit or position us better to enter the mood of talking to God in prayers. In the lives of most Bible-believing Christians, praise and worship rendered in modern style, often referred to as gospel, contemporary, jazz, country, etc., have become a preparer of souls and spirit to enter into prayer room. Most of our churches of today now have praise and worship as a very highly desired and can't-do-without item in their services, no matter the lengthiness or shortness of the time frame.

According to Felix Erondu in his recent booklet on prayer titled "Handle with Prayers," praise and worship give us access to the divine presence of God.[18] Being in the periphery of God at the prayer hour helps a whole lot. The psalmist knowledgeably informs us that God inhabits the praise of His people. In other words, God is literally in the house while praise and worship are in progress (Psalm 22:3).

Praise and worship are great facilitators of an excellent prayer forum. They often precede good and motivating prayer session. It is an energizer and a provider of grace to pray the more. Where there is praise or worship or both, blessings are bound to be released. Praying in a house where blessing is scheduled to be released is engaging in prayer that is effective, availing, and powerful.

The Lord speaks: "Let the people praise Me, then will be earth yield its increase, and God of heaven shall bless His people" (Psalm 67:5–7, NKJV) (paraphrased). Our Lord also is proclaimed to offer salvation and blessings to all who deliberately order their conversation aright before Him (Psalm 50:23). Praisers and worshippers surely are included in this group because God is excited whenever His people offer Him praise and worship. No better ordering of conversation can be presented unto God than praising and worshipping Him.

One Yoruba (language) adage expresses the underlying motivation in properly praising and worshipping God: *"Yin ni Yin ni, Ko tun ri omiran gba."* Translated, means: "When you offer praise and appreciation to a benefactor, he is induced to bless you more," and that is the scenario with God. We are pretty accustomed to the cliché when praises go up, blessings come down.

The foundation power of praise and worship resulting in a rich terrain of prayers answered is the appropriateness of the very act. God is a good and great Father He is, who provides all things richly unto us. I'm awed by His love and generosity toward us by spending five and half days to create resources for man so that by the time we arrive in creation on the sixth day, we would have lacked nothing. David expressed it beautifully, "It is a good thing to give thanks unto the LORD, and to sing praises unto thy name, O Most High" (Psalm 92:1, KJV).

Believers who look to enjoy successful prayer session must get praise and worship aboard the flight to the prayer mountain. They must dig deeper into thoughtfulness and exhume the praise of our God. Hearty praise emanates from candid thoughtfulness. Thoughtful people are more graced to handle better and more important things, and you know what? God's stuff are more important. And therefore, people given to prayers with the atmosphere decorated for results are more likely to receive important things and consideration from the Lord, who incidentally answers prayers.

Chris Oyakhlome was in tune with this indisputable reasoning: "Beside the fact that worship is a blessing in that it helps you to tune your spiritual attention to God's frequency, you give the Lord what He deserves when you worship Him."[19]

4. RIGHT PROCEDURE

Benny Hinn, sharing his experience in the efficacy of his prayer practice, has identified what he called "seven distinct steps to prayer"—confession, supplication, adoration, time of intimacy, intercession, thanksgiving, and praise.[20] He is tenacious with this ladder which he climbs often to a platform of success in prayer. To him, it is his expert procedure, the mode of approaching the throne of grace in prayers. He was resolute that doing it that way works, albeit for him. To others, he recommends the same.

As we grow in the Lord, we must attain skills at the altar of prayer with which we can articulate our communications with God in an intellectual-spiritual manner. To a good degree, this is individually developed by the help of the Holy

Spirit. To me, I see Benny Hinn's listing as components of prayers that must be effective, which I discussed in another chapter.

To "the young in faith," you cannot fret. As you submit to the Holy Spirit to lead and guide you in the place and into the mode of prayer, assessing your action in retrospect may have reflected some or all of Hinn's steps because we are led by the same Holy Spirit, even as Paul confirms the indefeasible dogma: One Lord, one faith, one baptism; One God and Father of all, who is over all and through all, and in you all (Ephesians 4:5–6). According to Nathaniel Bassey, "A true child of God never lacks structure in the place of prayer for the right expressions because the Holy Spirit is available to 'carry us' through."[21]

It is important to know that regardless of what channel you are routed to the altar, one procedure is unavoidable, and it must be underscored. Jesus pontificated: "And whatever you ask in My name, that I will do, that the Father may be glorified in the Son. If you ask anything in My name, I will do it" (John 14:13–14, NKJV). Done deal! We are offered this mention as an equivalent of a valid signature to a check. Automatic, it is money!

You may want to ask, what is the underlying power of this name that has been anointed to accompany our prayers unto God for an auto response? Searching further, God gave us the answer through the expression of joy and appreciation of what the beloved Son, Jesus, did by coming down as man to pay the price of reconciliation of men to the Father God. So, the Father took note of how He, being in the form of God, did not think it robbery to be equal with God but made Himself of no reputation and took upon Him a form of a servant and was made in the likeness of men... wherefore God has highly exalted Him...and that every tongue should confess that Jesus Christ is Lord, to the glory of God the Father (Philippians 2:6–11).

The name of Jesus is exciting to God. No wonder He calls Him beloved, and when legitimate requests are made with the mention of that sweet and loving name, God cannot turn away His hearing and response (Matthew 3:17, John 14:13). How blessed are we to be saved by and be identified with the Savior Jesus and His powerful name.

Attached to the power from God's side is ours because it is He (Christ) who saved us, and so by this act has become the first fruits of those who have been called and named into the family of God. With His name effectively voiced out of our mouths, we are trusted into a vantage position with God and obtain favor with man.

To the men redeemed by Jesus' own blood, the name symbolizes a divine connection. It is the Divine Universal Personal Identification Number (DUPIN) that generally but privately grants us access into the vault of God's immeasurable blessing.

5. INFILLING OF THE HOLY SPIRIT

Infilling of the Holy Spirit is a great facilitator of prayer; when a person is filled with the spirit, he is more enthused to do things of the spirit, for which praying is prime.

Please bear in mind that everyone who is born again has the Holy Spirit, for you cannot become a legitimate child of God without the work of the Holy Spirit done in your life. Having the Holy Ghost does not mean one is filled with the Holy Ghost. Receiving the Holy Ghost is one level, and being filled is another. We are encouragingly commanded to be filled with the Holy Ghost (Ephesians 5:17–21).

In order to be filled, there are certain steps of living that we must heed. Efforts must be applied to studying and storing the Word of God in our hearts, which the spirit will gradually feed on. We must stay in fellowship with fellow believers, knowing that iron sharpens iron. In other words, when good birds of the same feather flock together, they make one another better. Therefore, believers who fellowship together make each other better when each brings their spiritual gifts and enablement into the house of God to benefit all mutually. All these and many spiritual oblations that we attend to in fellowship result in the muscling up of the Holy Spirit, which, in turn, empowers and energizes us to take part in spiritual activities like praying with accessories of power and effectiveness.

Praying is a spiritual act that will not automatically

appeal to the flesh or an ordinary person. Deciding to go into the presence of the Lord would often use some help from the spirit man. Total surrender to the Lord by allowing the full takeover by the spirit of God is fundamentally useful, the absence of which, according to Will Malgo, often resulted in what he characterized as spiritual miscarriages.[22] He observed that despite our "preaching" and "prayers," many situations being confronted had not yielded because those who undertook the prayers had not completely surrendered their lives to the Lord, were crucified with Christ, or were willing to dedicate their whole life. He was convinced that, like Elijah, when one carries the Lord's burden completely in prayer, God will answer: "And the LORD heard the voice of Elijah; and the soul of the child came into him again, and he revived (1 Kings 17:22, KJV). Imagine the new atmosphere when Elijah took the child and brought him down the stairs from the chambers to the mother and said, "See, thy son liveth" (verse 23, KJV). It was joy unhindered in the house of the godly.

It is for results such as these that, as a baby believer, one must strive to start the walk of faith right, making oneself accountable to some older in faith who can lovingly and patiently encourage you at the beginning so that gradually you can mature from the stage of being a baby who loves soft and easy ways of walking with God. Being gradually fed must lead to a stronger build that will begin to make us determined to persevere in the place of prayer.

In what specific ways does the active Holy Spirit help

us to be more prayerful? Generally, in His assignments unto us as a resident, He is a helper, a teacher, a comforter, and an empowerer. He encourages and helps us to pray (John 14:16–18), supplies extra power and energy to pray amongst other functioning (Acts 1:8, James 5:16b), and sometimes substitutes for us in the place and time of prayer (Romans 8:26). He prays to the Lord in languages that human intellect may not have understanding. Those kinds of prayers are very effective because the Holy Spirit that knows the mind of the Father toward us is praying to the same.

It is very helpful to be filled with the spirit, and for the reasons shared, I believe you need to. Nothing is holding you back from becoming a vibrant prayer warrior and intercessor.

6. RIGHT PERSON OR PEOPLE

Hanging out with the right people can be a great asset in the quest for enjoying the bliss of powerful and vibrant prayers. People are not the same. Churches are not the same. Even among the "born again," many will never be on the same level of faith and operation. In any spiritual functioning that we are called into, being with the right group is a potent catalyst for attaining excellence.

The wisdom of positive contagion was shared with us that iron sharpens iron, so does a man sharpen the countenance of his friend (Proverbs 27:17). This wisdom implies that in the field of prayers, being in the house with prayer warriors or those given to intercession (intercessors) cannot hurt you. In their midst, you will be energized and aligned with the right prayer mood.

Apostle Matthew transcribes for us a word from his Master that where more than one is gathered together in the name of Jesus, God will be in the midst (Matthew 18:20). Therefore, a gathering of those who know and focus on the Lord is a rich fellowship of likeminded people where prayers can produce desirable results since the one who answers prayer is in the house. The benefit of agreement is an added power that cannot be over-emphasized nor justifiably jettisoned (cf. verse 19).

Those who are serious about getting the best from their prayer venture must avoid a gathering where sin is given space and made comfortable. Sin is a power neutralizer to prayer. There is a reason why in Psalm 1, the Lord cautions us to not indulge in walking in the counsel of the ungodly, nor stand in the way of sinners or mount the seat of the scornful. These stances would not help us in prayer. A gathering that would enjoy God's favor in the place of prayer and intercession must be committed to dealing with sin. Remember, if we regard iniquity in our hearts, God says He will not hear us (Psalm 66:18).

That is why prayer conductors in a fellowship must encourage humility before God, coming with a contrite heart, encouraging people to lay it all down before the altar, and appropriate the cleansing power of the blood of Jesus into our struggles and sins before we start the active proposition of praying.

In the family setting, I encourage you to operate in the same mindset. Family members must endeavor to create an atmosphere of spiritual decency and righteousness so that our devotions and prayers may be fruitful as the Lord promises the godly (verse 3).

CHAPTER 4:

PRAYER AS A TOOL

Satan's sojourn on earth has turned the life's journey of man into a warfare that can only be successfully fought by tools divinely supplied by God. Those who will eventually live in New Jerusalem must be armed with these weapons of war, which are not canal but are mighty through God, for bringing down principalities and powers of darkness, of which prayer is preferred.

Prayer has been given unto believers as a tool that is well-sharpened and trained by divine ordination and is handily useful in diverse ways. What prayer can do, what it can accomplish, and the benefits following its execution have made it one of the most effective weapons in the hand of a believer. And why will it not be, with the fact that in prayer, we are asking the Omnipotent, the Omniscient, and the Omnipresent to come and be on our side? Granting such a request constitutes the most advantageous position on earth.

1. A TOOL OF PREVENTION

An old adage proclaims that prevention is better than cure. In our modern-day practice of counseling and administering of people, we are urged to be proactive rather than reactive. The mindset of birthing prayer as a tool of prevention is an excellent disposition—it is economical and superiorly effective. It is cheaper and less laborious to prevent a disaster than nurse it. It is less painful to live healthily than seek healing from whatever avenue. All these examples emphasize an urge to a believer that prayer as a tool of prevention is an adopted practice of the wise.

Jesus practically teaches us that prayer can avert troubles, disasters, pain, sorrow, death (physical or spiritual), and anything undesirable. In the legendary Lord's Prayer, a model given unto us by the One whose name we must pray to get results, He expressed, "Lead us not into temptation" (Matthew 6:13a, KJV). This means that it is desirable and effective to pray off an occurrence that we do not desire. Evil can be fenced off. As a matter of fact, the second part of verse 13, in one connotation, depicts this thought: Deliver us from evil. While it may mean rescuing us out of the bad occurrences that we are in, it may also, on the other hand, mean that Lord does not allow evil occurrences to befall us.

For instance, as Jesus timed encounter with the cross was fastly drawing closer, He urged His disciples to pray that they enter not into the realm of temptation (Luke 22:39–43). He foresaw that in the next few hours, the atmosphere would be ripe for all types of hardships and potential bad actions and reactions. The betrayer, the soldiers, the chief priests, and the Pharisees, who had stood up against Him with one unified purpose of getting rid of Him, were all in the horizon. They were around the corner to arrest and kill. There was no telling precisely how vast the damage would be. Sometimes, a projected bloodless coup may take a new twist, and heads may start to roll. The atmosphere was cloudy with possibilities of tragedies. And so, Christ went into prayers and urged the disciples to dig deep. Though some things have been written, and those will happen regardless, prayers could avert many potential evils and disasters that are not scripted. The text would later hint about the inability of those men to stay strong in the place of prayer. They were overcome with the focus on the brewing troubles rather than on fixing their hearts on the God who is able to temper situations and things.

We may never be able to measure what impact, if any, of how the inability to pray affected the aggravation of the series of events that followed thereafter. But we know firsthand that prayer does make a big difference. It is anointed to prevent evil or mitigate damages where things have been scripted to occur regardless. Jesus' second coming to earth is an event that must happen but would be preceded by very difficult and tumultuous times. Knowing this and that prayer can help, He encouraged those who would be alive at that time to be watchful and prayerful so that they could escape all the heaviness of the impending doom, such as dissipation, anxieties, and tribulations (Luke 21:34–35). It is very important because this could determine if they go with Christ to glory or fall short and end in perdition.

Prayers can prevent the enemies of our souls from devouring us. Apostle Peter says,

> *Be sober, be vigilant [be watchful, be prayerful], because your adversary the devil, as a roaring lion, walketh about, seeking whom he may devour;*
>
> *Whom resist steadfast in the faith, knowing that the same afflictions are accomplished in your brethren that are in the world.*
>
> **1 Peter 5:8–9 (KJV)**

In contacting diseases and sicknesses, prayer can be a ready tool. Jesus postulates: "And these signs shall follow them that believe; […] if they drink any deadly thing, it shall not hurt them..." (Mark 16:17a–18a, KJV) Contamination and poison from bad foods and drinks can cause sickness and disease. Therefore, praying on our foods as a trained believer kills the germs and contamination and makes the food safe for good health.

Apostle Paul, writing to the Corinthians and believers in general, stressed the importance of blessing and consecrating the foods that we eat while he was giving a discourse on the food sacrificed to idols. Though a few other lessons could be learned from the exposition (1 Corinthians chapters 8 and 10), however, at this particular junction, we can deduce that if we need to eat a food regardless of the source, we are safer blessing it before we do. By so doing, we know we are edged up against anything undesirable.

Prayer can forestall death. The psalmist proclaimed in prayer—"I shall not die, but live, and declare the works of the LORD" (Psalm 118:17, KJV). In Acts chapter 12, we read of how the New Testament church members prayed to retrieve the life of Peter from death at the hands of the enemies of the church. It was an inciting account. They had previously arrested James, the general superintendent of the church, and had him killed. Seeing that no one in the church raised an eyebrow and that many of the Jews were actually pleased, they proceeded to take Peter and put him in incarceration until after the Passover so that they could have him killed. But thanks goodness, the church rose up against the vile of Herod and his master Satan. In ceaseless prayers, the church gathered and stood. The night before he would have been killed, the Lord sent an angel down from heaven and miraculously saved and delivered Peter. He came to present himself to them where they were still interceding for him. They all thanked God for amazingly answering their prayers and restoring Peter back to his full life and ministry.

Prayer is a preventer of all that is not good. As a child of God, pray preventively. In the song "What a Friend We Have in Jesus," one of the verses enlightened us that we often suffer needlessly because many of us have not learned to bring everything to God in prayer. Our God is not only interested in helping to remove the bad; He, actually, is willing to prevent the bad from happening if we are proactive in our meditations and prayers.

In our world of today, whereby family problems abound, bad relationships could be nipped in the bud just as good and successful marriages can be built upon the foundation of prayers.

2. A TOOL OF MAINTENANCE

Where something is good and beautiful, it is a legitimate human desire and propensity to keep it up and standardized, maintaining the great status quo. For instance, when you buy a brand-new car, certain maintenance recommendations are given to ensure the car runs very well for a long time. Maintenance schedules are constructed. In similar manner, a good life, family, and situation conditions that bear on us are kept in great condition by asking God for help through prayers and obediently walking with and relating with God. Prayers and close walk with God will be to a born-again life what an oil change is to a new car, and as a matter of fact, not just a newly born-again life or a brand-new car only but all lives and all cars. Solomon, in his wisdom reminiscing about the essentiality of preserving a good condition, expressed earnestly how a righteous man should endeavor never to fall or, better still, not in the sight of the wicked because the wicked would make a mockery of him (Proverbs 25:26). The righteous can keep standing and continue to do well; that would be the desire of the heart of

God who loves to see the prosperity of His children.

The situation in the country of Judah after Abijah the king passed on and Asa resumed rulership was a classic example of how prayers and seeking the face of God can be a powerful tool of maintaining a peaceful status quo in the land (cf. 2 Chronicles chapter 14). Abijah, who in the last ten years of his reign had enjoyed an unqualified peace, passed the baton to his son Asa. So, the heir apparent was inheriting peace in the land. How smart he was; he vowed to maintain the peace in the country. He accordingly went to work, knowing that having peace with God is a precondition of living a peaceful life. Therefore, in 2 Chronicles 14:2 (KJV), we are told, "And Asa did that which was good and right in the eyes of the LORD his God." From this report, it was certain that he had an obvious relationship with God. Only those who are genuinely related to God can refer to Him as their Lord and God. That is a confident personal expression of certainty of relationship.

Having cemented his own personal stand with the Lord, he proceeded to take actions that would bear on the nation's solid relationship with God. He cleared the national congregational altars of strange gods and removed the abominable high places, broke down the images, and cut down the groves. These were national emblems of idolatry that were irritating to the Lord. Taking these steps secured for the land a guaranteed pleasant happy disposition from the Lord. Following, he issued an edict that the whole nation must seek the Lord, God of their father, and obey the law and the commandment of God. He went beyond Jerusalem, the capital city, and cleansed the remaining cities and towns of all abominable objects that can bring displeasure of the Lord (verses 3 to 6).

Result: the peace that was handed over to him remained and actually thrived better. He was able to expand and prolong the peaceful and secured season. He amassed a great army for security and defense. This, for him, was wise. We know as wise children of God that we must be sober and vigilant because we have an adversary who is bothered by the grace we enjoy. We know that when things are good, the enemy of our souls will try to rock the peace. Thanks to God, our rock of defense, the sun, and the shield: the defender of all who have made Him their refuge.

In the confines of this peace, the enemy came roaring—Zerah the Ethiopian—arrayed more than a million war chariots against Asa and Judah. Even though he had built a relatively large army that could get into the lines, nevertheless, he called upon the Lord, the Man of War, who doesn't have to rely on numbers to secure victory over His enemies. He is the same God who once decimated 185,000 powerful Assyrian soldiers through one angel (2 Kings 19:35). King Asa understood that many might rely on horses and more on chariots, but towing the path of those who trust in the name of the Lord was always more victory assured.

He prayed: "[...] help us, O LORD our God; for we rest

on thee, and in thy name we go against this multitude. O LORD, thou art our God; let no man prevail against thee" (2 Chronicles 14:11b, KJV).

And the Lord responded and smote the Ethiopians before Asa and Judah. The hosts of the enemy were routed, and the peace of the land was preserved. Following, the spirit of the Lord spoke through Azariah, son of Oded, confirming how He honors those who chose to draw close to Him in life walk and prayer, with His own presence and saving power (2 Chronicles chapter 15). He was commended and further encouraged to not relent: "Be ye strong therefore and let not your hands be weak: for your work shall be rewarded" (2 Chronicles 15:7, KJV). With that encouraging *Rhema*, he proceeded to take further actions that brought the nation even closer to the Lord. The corresponding result: the land enjoyed peace for the thirty-five years of his reign.

His prayer and close relationship with the Lord extended a ten-year peace package in to thirty-five years of tranquility, plus physical security reinforcement.

This can be maintained if you have a great thing going on in your life or family or in your church, village, town, or city. Seek the Lord in prayers and closer relationship; like He did for Asa, He will do the same for you. He gives peace like no human can. My God can be trusted.

3. A TOOL OF SOLUTION

Like the mathematicians rely on the "almighty formula" to solve even the most complex of quadratic equations, so prayer, for all who have come to understand its mysterious power, can be a single source of answers to all questions and solutions to all challenges and problems life may throw at us.

All things we are told are possible to all who believe. For God, we have been foretold, nothing shall be impossible (Luke 1:37). These tested and proven declarations have been validated all through the ages by people who, through prayers (and sometimes with fasting), have moved the hands of God to do great marvelous works and have engaged His eyes to run to and from the length and breadth of the cosmos delivering with miraculous precision. Prayer presents a tool of proof of the incredible that God can do, does, and has done times without number. It is then not surprising that the wise Job of the ancient times declared that he would always turn to God in times of need (Job 5:8–9).

Jesus, while on earth, did a lot of eye-popping works and performed a lot of stunning miracles. Prayers were the underscores. In Mark chapter 9, in particular, was the deliverance of a demon-possessed boy. The issue that faced the father of the boy was catalytic. It was bizarre. To have a son so struck with a number of very heavy blows for a parent was very challenging. Count—demonically possessed, dumb, led anywhere, and battered, causing him to foam (probably epileptic), gnashing his teeth agonizingly turning pale after being thoroughly beaten up. For the boy, but more for the parent, this was a problem of a special type and size that no one would pray for.

This family was devastated and a parasite in the neighborhood and the entire city. Perhaps the boy had to be fetched in places where the parents had felt and experienced heavy shame. So, this man needed a solution that only God, in His very special grace, can offer. And as God's mercy would be available on this very day, Jesus Christ was in the neighborhood.

The cry for a solution on this day as even desperate the boy probably having been just cast into fire or water in an attempt to completely annihilate him. God just had to intervene. "If thou canst believe, all things are possible to him that believeth" (Mark 9:23, KJV), Jesus said. That was the closest to anything that would be helpful. And straightaway, the father of the boy bellowed, with tears, "Lord, I believe, help thou mine unbelief" (Mark 9:24b, KJV). Remember that shortly before this encounter, Jesus had just been transfigured on a mountain with Peter, James, and John, and a lot of prayers and spiritual empowerment had taken place. With this recent background in place, Jesus charged the spirit, ordering him to come out of the boy and never to enter therein. The resistance was so potent that the spirit made a lasting attempt to intimidate Jesus while renting the boy sore, jerking him badly and dropping him lifeless while leaving him. Thank God, Jesus, with all authority and power, could not disobey nor lastingly resist.

Jesus was in charge and held up the boy, life and health fully restored. Later in private confines with the disciples, we know the basis upon which types of miracles and wonders can happen. The disciple wowed by the magnitude of the miracle just had to know why they could not come close and how it was easy for their Master, Jesus. The code was revealed—only by prayer and fasting can such wondrous and marvelous miracles take place.

Therefore, take it home, beloved: prayers accompanied by fasting, sometimes as one is led by the spirit, will be a solution to problems and issues of difficult degrees. Are you faced with a uniquely strange problem or issue? Seek God in prayer and fasting; you are close to a solution. Prayer (and fasting) has been given to a believer as a tool of providing a solution to any problem of life, for that matter.

4. A TOOL TO FIGHT/WEAPON OF WAR

The very moment a man is born again or gives his life to Christ, he adds a status to his life, that of being a target for the arch enemy of the redeemed soul, Satan. Satan originally had an issue with God, his Creator. This started when, in arrogance, he rebelled against God, wanting to ascend to the place of God and attempting to usurp power and prominence (Isaiah 14:12–17). For which he was stopped and thereafter cast down from heaven and given a sentence upon his head that at the end of the age, he would be hell bound. Knowing that he has no chance of redemption because he lacks the grace of repentance, he chose to henceforth antagonize anything that God stands for. None other would supersede Jesus, the beloved Son, and all of God's redeemed children through Christ. Having attempted to stop Christ and having been unable to, he resolved to fight every believer to his last pint of blood.

That is why the minute you become a real member of the family of God, Satan has you in his list of potential targets to wage war on. The Lord, our Father, knew this well, and He has set up a secured defense apparatus and security for all who truly belong to Him. But to be untouchable, we have a part to play.

First, God wants us to know and be aware of the current situations. He wants us not to be ignorant that we have a potent enemy in Satan. He tells us through Apostle Peter, "Be sober, be vigilant; your adversary Satan lurks around seeking whom to devour, whom you must resist (1 Peter 5:8, KJV) (paraphrased). To be sober means to be of full consciousness and knowledge of things around you. When you add the word "vigilant" to sober, you deduce an awareness that has no crack. So, God says to know that there is an enemy that is coming after you. Our Lord expects that the awareness of this fact spurs actions that will safeguard. The heightened awareness becomes more prolific when you add the information supplied by Apostle John (John 10:10a)—the arch enemy is coming around us for at least one of all of the three purposes: steal, kill, or destroy. Knowing all these means that not only can we not be careless, but we must be poised for a fight in case he draws too close or even attempt to touch us.

Because of the force and the fury with which he may attack, God commands us to "be strong in the Lord and in the power of His might. Put on the whole armor of God, that you may be able to stand the wiles of the devil..." (Ephesians 6:10–11, NKJV) But also because of his tricky nature of attacking his designated enemies, God wants us sometimes to be wise as a serpent and be watchful in the place of prayer. Satan as an accuser of the brethren (Revelation 12:10), a lair (John 8:44), the old serpent (Revelation 12:9), evil one (1 John 5:19), adversary (1 Peter 5:8), the great dragon (Revelation 12:9), and the devil (Revelation 12:9) demands all in the arsenal to fight. He is such a potent force that cannot be taken nonchalantly.

The real issue is that the devil is not always a physical enemy, but his assault on us most often will definitely leave a physical scar because our whole life is a combination of physical and spiritual. This implies that we must be prepared and equipped to fight him, mostly in the spiritual realm. Therefore, the Lord educates us that the weapons needed to fight Satan and overcome him are neither physical nor carnal: "(For the weapons of our warfare are not carnal, but mighty through God to the pulling down of strong holds;) casting down imaginations..." (2 Corinthians 10:4–5a, KJV) This implies you cannot go out looking to shoot or box, jab or hit the devil. You've got to be prepared to attack him in the place of prayer, resorting to harnessing the entire spiritual prowess that can tactically deal with the spiritual dimensions of Satan and his power.

It is because of the realm dimension of the engagements that altercations with the devil by believers are referred to as warfare. In the opinion of Erondu, which is very consistent with the derivation of straight understanding of scripture, Christian life is warfare.

> *The fact is, we are at war, and what we see or hear are results of invisible wars raging all over the world. The battle takes place in the spirit realm but results in physical outcome. You see, we cannot be deluded because of the outcomes that are physical to feel that we would deal with issues in that sense.*[23]

God plainly tells us the things that we see are controlled by the forces that we cannot see with our physical eyes (2 Corinthians chapter 4).

This is the summary reason why prayer has assumed a primarily important and inescapable role of combating the forces of darkness as wars are waged relentlessly against the children of God. I love that gospel hymn: "Christian seek not yet repose. / Hear thy guardian angel say. / Thou art in the midst of foes. / Watch and pray."[24] If indeed we obtain victory in the place of prayer, i.e., on our knees, then it is a good expression to retort: prayer is an effective instrument or tool of fighting and warring.

When David confidently expressed that it was the Lord who trained his fingers to fight and his hands to war, most assuredly, he had been met in the place of prayer. As a man notoriously reputed for praising and worshipping God, that he was a man given to prayer cannot be successfully challenged; for even the most inarticulate understands that a man who founds himself in the very presence of God via worship and praise is readily in the comfort zone of prayer that can never go amiss. That close to God is a level of fellowship unparalleled.

5. A TOOL FOR GUIDANCE

As we live our lives, believers need God's guidance to ensure perfect progress along life journeys. Sometimes, we get to junctions where we are open to alternative choices; in those instances, a specific guidance as to where to go or what to prefer can be of immeasurable value. Such a guide can be obtained through asking God in prayers.

The steps of a good man or a child of God are ordered by the Lord (Psalm 37:23). The same psalmist beseeched the Lord: "Shew me thy ways, O LORD; teach me thy paths. Lead me in thy truth, and teach me: for thou art the God of my salvation; on thee do I wait all the day" (Psalm 25:4–5, KJV). "Who is the man that fears the LORD? Him shall He teach in the way He chooses" (Psalm 25:12, NKJV).

In prayer, the will of God for a man is revealed, and as he walks those ways, he becomes prosperous and systematically fulfilled.

After Jesus had ascended to heaven and Judas Iscariot had lost his estate and his place had become void, the apostles needed to replace him. They needed guidance. They resorted to praying.

> *And they appointed two, Joseph called Barsabas, who was surnamed Justus, and Matthias. And they prayed, and said, Thou, Lord, which knowest the hearts of all men, shew whether of these two thou hast chosen, that he may take part of this ministry and apostleship, from which Judas by transgression fell, that he might go to his own place. And they gave forth their lots; and the lot fell upon Matthias; and he was numbered with the eleven apostles [to make up a total of twelve].*
>
> **Acts 1:23–26 (KJV)**

In this situation, through prayer, God guided them by way of casting lots to make a choice between two people to replace Judas.

In 1 Samuel chapter 30, at the season when David was in Diaspora awaiting his installation as a replacement of Saul, he encountered a devastating loss of his family and properties from the band of the Amalekites. He became extremely troubled and needed to make a decision whether to go after his enemies. Understanding how important it was to do things according to the mind of God, decided to ask God for guidance: "And David inquired at the LORD [asked the Lord in prayer], saying, Shall I pursue after this troop? shall I overcome them? And he [God] answered him, Pursue: for thou shall surely overtake, and without fail recover all" (1 Samuel 30:8, KJV).

Following this directive guide, David and his band pursued the enemy and not only recovered everything that originally belonged to him but also plundered their bands. According to the guidance provided, David got all back and was fully restored. No plans in our lives work better than the ones we were guided to execute. The ways of the Lord are perfect.

I charge you to remember to go to God at those moments in your life when you are faced with choices, and there appears not to be a clear path. God is very interested in guiding you. Don't feel that you are not a pastor or prophet or an elder. God is no respecter of persons. Approach Him wholeheartedly and speak to Him as you would your father and friend, and believe that He hears you and is interested in guiding you. I assure you, He will give you a reply by any means that you can relate with and understand. It may be through dream, audible voice in your ears, silent voice in your heart, through a man of God, or by clean circumstance that gives you peace confirmed by the Holy Spirit in you.

6. TOOL OF INITIATION

Prayer is useful to birth into existence a provision. Is there a vision, a desire, a wish, a contemplation, a plan, or a need that must be met? Going to the Lord in prayer can always originate the provision. With the prayer of initiation, things are brought into physical existence or realization.

Hannah needed a child; she prayed to the Lord for several years. Neither she nor her husband, Elkanah, doubted the fact that only God could give a child. She did not give up asking God in prayers. Eventually, on the occasion of yet another visit to Shiloh, the problem got to her pretty good, "And she was in bitterness of soul, and prayed unto the LORD, and wept sore" (1 Samuel 1:10, KJV). "And it came to pass, as she continued praying before the LORD, that Eli marked her mouth" (1 Samuel 1:12, KJV).

> *And Hannah answered and said, No, my lord, I am a woman of sorrowful spirit: I have not drunk neither wine nor strong drink, but have poured out my soul before the LORD.*
>
> *Count not thine handmaid for a daughter of Belial: for out of abundance of my complaint and grief have I spoken hitherto.*
>
> *Then Eli answered and said, Go in peace: and the God of Israel grant thee thy petition that thou have asked of him.*
>
> *And she said, Let thine handmaid find grace in thy sight.*
>
> **1 Samuel 1:15–18a (KJV)**

The child needed could only be given of God. She did not give up in the place of prayer until the Lord decided to answer. She got her first child and son. Later on, the Lord would bless her with five more children. Prayer was the initiation tool. She birthed the children with ceaseless prayer unto God.

What do we lack? We must ask God. The Lord himself wants us to ask for whatever we lack and really need to have. If we lack wisdom, God says to ask Him; He usually gives liberally, and He won't withhold (James 1:5). Jeremiah in the book of Lamentations declared: "'The LORD is my portion,' says my soul, 'Therefore I hope in Him!'" (Lamentations 3:24, NKJV) Paul assures us of the eternal promise of our Father at His willingness to supply all of our needs according to His riches in glory through Christ Jesus (Philippians 4:19). The bottom line is with prayers, provision can be birthed, no matter what it is. Pray until provision is released.

From a child to money, to victory over enemies, to deliverance from slavery, to delivery from the mouth of lions, to release out of a fiery furnace, to commutation of death by hanging to life, to deliverance from demonic inhabitation, to healings from diverse diseases, to raising up from the dead, to restoration of fortune, saving of unsaved souls, etc., prayer, over the times, had come in handy as tool of initiation. God had met tons of needs. He still does today if you can call upon Him.

7. A TOOL FOR HEALING AND MEDICATION

One of the most intriguing heart desires of God for all of His children is the enjoyment of good health as we live our lives. Hear the word of the Lord "Beloved, I wish above all things that thou mayest prosper and be in health, even as thy soul prospereth" (3 John 2, KJV). In this pronouncement, an age-long fact is revealed. The soul of a child of God is prosperous, ipso facto. The one who belongs to God, he (his soul) is eternally secured in all things and in all realms. Understanding the fullness of such security and completeness, God prays and envisions that His children enjoy good health physically, just as his soul.

Of course, we know that since the fall of man (in Genesis chapter 3), man is subject to physical depreciation and deterioration ultimately (though our outward man perishes, but our inner man gets stronger by the day—2 Corinthians 4:16), though the inner man of a believer would continue to rise in strength by the day. However, and in spite, God's mind for His own is to be in health and live well. How can this be achieved? Through healing and body replenishing whenever the body caves in under pressure of ill health. For sure, our God knows that the body of sin may not altogether escape sickness and ailment, and He said through the mouth of Apostle James,

Is any among you afflicted? let him pray. […] Is any sick among you? let him call the elders of the church, and let them pray over him, anointing him with oil in the name of the Lord:

And the prayer of faith shall save the sick, and the Lord shall raise him up; and if he had committed sins, they shall be forgiven him.

Confess your faults one to another, and pray one for another, that ye may be healed. The effectual fervent prayer of the righteous man availeth much.

James 5:13–16 (KJV)

Clearly and unambiguously, the Lord in this text states that prayer is a tool with which sickness and ailment can be battled. They have attacked the body of a child of God to break it down, committed to obliteration, but God, willing our body to live, gives us prayer as a perfect antidote to sickness. Prayer, therefore, is the medication for a believer at the time of physical breakdown. In the event that the body is attacked by sickness, God stipulates that the prayers offered in faith will raise the sick from his infirmity. Yes, sicknesses can identify prayer as an uprooter of ailments. It responds to its operation. Hear David: "The strangers shall fade away, and be afraid out of their close places" (Psalm 18:45, KJV). The ultimate desire of God is that sickness will have no comfort zone in our bodies, and through the power of spoken prayers, God has always achieved His purposes through those who care to do what He recommends for us.

A medical poll reported by Duke Medical School revealed that there is a positive correlation between healing and prayers. Those who were being prayed for got better faster than those who were not. A researcher and writer Tom Knox, a one-time atheist who became a regular worshipper after doing in-depth study of the medical benefits of faith, confessed that he was astonished by what he discovered: "Over the past thirty years, a growing and largely unnoticed body of scientific work shows religious belief is medically, socially, and psychologically beneficial."[25] He concludes by declaring that the proof of the power of prayer is overwhelming!

On a national platform, as much as there are forces that have been fighting to box out God from the arena, yet we see how gracious the Lord is when He gives a proposition of way out of the woods to a nation that is sick or in trouble. He compassionately demanded: "Let My people who are called by *My* name humble themselves and *pray* and *seek* My face, and turn from their wicked ways, then will I hear from heaven, and will forgive their sin and heal their land" (2 Chronicles 7:14, NKJV). It's amazing that a group and collection of people can be so dramatically affected by prayers. Prayer is a force like a good wind that brings nothing but good. Good things happen when people pray. Conversely, no one can guarantee what will happen when the watch men and women are overtaken by sleepiness and spiritual decadence.

8. TOOL FOR CONTROLLING NATURE

Believers armed with the powerful fallout of prayer don't go about messing with nature just for the fun of it. Nature, cosmos, the weather, seasons, and all of those natural phenomena are created of God, and as they exist and function in their own rights and turfs, they help man to fulfill his purpose and destiny. And that is the way we will take it.

However, there have been instances (and will always be) when nature as it works its course became a disturbance to the peace of the men who have been given power and authority over it. The maxim that divinely governs interrelationship between all creatures with certain powers is that none should pose a threat unto another. Two servants of the same powerful master should not disturb each other when they are both on duty for their master.

On occasions when this had happened, man armed with power and authority from God had always taken charge. Please remember that we have been mandated to have dominion over all other formed things (Genesis 1:26–28).

For instance, Jesus was voyaging on the sea en route to a retreat with His disciples when suddenly a storm decided to show up raging (Luke 8:22–25). Though Jesus was napping and would not experience firsthand the severity of the storm, however, the disciples were panicky and all shaken up. They were kind of even more disturbed because in the midst of their "woes," master Jesus was asleep obviously untouched by the confusion that was rife. Nevertheless, when He was woken up, He was not to be denied by a creation of His own hands. He was the master, to begin with. Getting up, He rebuked the wind, causing the raging storm to subside.

Elijah was set to wage a war on Ahab and his wicked and ungodly people. He would need to get their attention, and he chose to employ weather. He commanded (decreed) the rain to cease for three years. The man of God was on a mission for God, and rain would prayerfully be commandeered to his favor (1 King chapter 17). The success of this proven prowess of prayer over nature was later alluded to by Apostle James of the New Testament church. In his treatise teaching and encouraging us on the power of prayers, he reminded or pointed to us how Elijah, a human being like you and me, prayerfully commanded that rain to cease for three years, and rain obeyed; it did not fall (James 5:17–18).

Many modern-day people have not let this feat be restricted to the biblical times only. While I was growing up in Nigeria, many a time in our church, we had prayed for rain to fall when there was a prolonged dearth and crops and plants needed to flourish. On the other hand, there were times when we had open-air revival services, and rain would threaten to dismantle the gospel mission for the day. On numerous occasions, prayers offered passionately and in faith had turned back the rain and allowed the revival services to proceed as scheduled.

Pastor Yemi Ayodele of the Church of Nations in Houston, Texas, was our guest preacher at Our Savior's Church, Houston, during the 2014 Calvary. He testified to how, in his revivals in South America, rain was prayed on hold that revival services might hold without disturbance. Reinhardt Bunke, the massive crowd puller in Nigeria, gave testimonies on similar prayer escapades.

My grandmother, now gone to be with the Lord, was a prayer-powerful woman of God. She founded and directed the Christ Apostolic Church (CAC) in her hometown of Ilu Omoba in Nigeria. She shared with us on one occasion when she had to travel on foot to Ado-Ekiti to meet her spiritual leader: Apostle Ayo Babalola.[26] In this particular reported episode, two distinctive miracles happened. The journey, which would normally take about six hours, took her less than two hours. This was a miracle of distance retraction. Unbelievable! Furthermore, while she was en route, rain started to fall, but no water touched her. As she proceeded, there was a dry sphere around her all through her journey. It was amazing, but that is what prayer offered in faith can do. Not only will provisions, victory, healing, etc., be brought to life through the power of prayer, even weather and nature will not escape prayer in operation.

CHAPTER 5:

FORMS OF PRAYER

It is wisdom to learn the ways of those who succeeded in the field that we cannot avoid. No Christian reaches his potential without prayer. Even Jesus was not exempt. Studying the pastimes of the patriarchs has revealed the many alternative ways to entreat God. Those great men of faith were never limited by circumstances. In emulating them, we will not fail where they succeeded. For God never changes: He is the same yesterday, today, and forever.

Let's identify different ways to pray and forms of prayer:

1. PRAISE AND WORSHIP

The thesis being expounded here is that there are instances when praise and worship and expressions of appreciation and adoration without formal prayer would bring tremendous blessings and breakthroughs. In these instances, it is perfect to conclude that such expressions without prayers are forms of prayer on their own because they do the jobs of actual prayers.

Let's begin by looking at a few instances in scripture where such fits the take: Though praise and worship have been defined and seen as a door opener or a grantor of access to the divine presence of God, however on the stronger side, it has actually from time to time assumes the status of prayer.

Psalm 67:5–7. The psalmist confirms that when people are moved to praise the Lord, the earth yields her increase. Blessings come upon God's people. Others (without) who see the effect of the praise and what windfall it has brought would begin to be amazed at God's doing for His people.

Acts 16:25. Paul and Silas were praying and singing at Philippi in the jailhouse. Suddenly came earthquakes; the foundation of the prison shook, and the door automatically opened; chains fell off them, suicide was averted, and souls were saved (whole family of the guard) and baptized. They were released with honors. In this instance, singing hymns and praise functioned in the place of prayers, and unprecedented miracles happened.

Joshua 5:13–6:27. A shout after the Israelites had circled Jericho seven times on the seventh day, following intense blowing of the rams' horns by the priests, resulted in the monumental fall of the wall of Jericho. Again, these acts of unusual marching praise and instrumental music were a form of prayer that got answered with downing of the monumental wall.

2 Chronicle 20:20–23. Sequel to singing and praising God, the Lord went in to fight the battle and operated a triangle of routing of the nations of Ammon, Moab, and Mount Seir. Earlier in the chapter, the spirit of the Lord, through Jahaziel, a descendant of Asaph, had told them that the battle was His and that the enemy would be obliterated. However, Jehoshaphat ordered praise, and the war was fought by God following. Again, like a divine response to the like of a national forty-day fasting and prayer marathon, the Lord did not only rout this cartel of foes, but He actually blessed His people with massive spoils of silver, gold, and riches, so excessive that they could not take all. Again, the summation of all that was done here with no iota of formal prayers amounted to a form of prayer.

On the praise night of Calvary 2013 at Our Savior's Church in Houston, we had structured the praise sector to end at around 9:30 p.m. so that Archbishop Powerson, the guest preacher, would cap the evening with about twenty minutes message and then dismiss the service, but somehow, the Holy Ghost decided to veer the affairs into a different direction, with the praise changing gear into a higher octave and continued till midnight. Nobody could leave. The glory of the Lord thickly filled the sanctuary, and the Lord began to reveal many breakthroughs and blessings that were poured upon people who were high with the praise of God. No formal prayers were said on that night compared to the other nights, but the revealed works and wonders of the Lord on that night were unparalleled.

The praise and worship on that night assumed the status of some kind of high-powered prayers that brought a lot of manifestations of the power of God, working in the troubling affairs of His children's lives.

2. DECREEING OR SPEAKING FORTH (MATTHEW 18:18)

The perfect models for these kinds of prayer are given by God and Jesus. In Genesis, the first chapter, we read a number of times the phrases: "And God said…"; "Let there be light…"; "Let there be a firmament in the midst of the waters…"; Let the earth bring forth grass…"; "[...] and it was so…" (Genesis 1:3–25, KJV) In the gospel, according to Mark, we found the following declaration by Jesus: "When Jesus saw their faith, he said unto the sick of the palsy, Son thy sins be forgiven thee" (Mark 2:5). "Arise, and take thy bed, and go thy way into thine house" (Mark 2:11, KJV). "Stretch forth thine hand..." (Mark 3:5, KJV) "Peace, be still..." (Mark 4:39, KJV) "Come out of the man, thou unclean spirit" (Mark 5:8, KJV). "Talitha cumi; [...] Damsel, I say unto thee, arise" (Mark 5:41b, KJV).

Following all these decrees and declarations spoken forth were miracles of profound proportions. Sickness, demons, and living and nonliving things were responding and obeying His words just like creations were springing up and forming at the sound of the word of God. These kinds of words released in decree or declaration or simply speaking forth resulted in unbelievable deliverance, healing, banishing, and diverse miracles. Words spoken in His manner have become prayers that are spontaneously answered in the manner of Jesus' proclamation of Matthew 18:18 (KJV): "Whatsoever ye shall bind on earth shall be bound in heaven: and whatsoever ye shall loose on earth shall be loosed in heaven." That God and Jesus the Savior used this form of prayer shows us the status of any that will be engraved to operate these forms of prayer. In their impeccable nature and on their lofty platform, they both exemplify what a level one can reach spiritually to be able to flow in decree, declaration, and speaking forth. We know that God is the Creator-Maker of all things, the One with no beginning and end, the uncaused cause of all causes, the One who speaks and automatically comes to pass, Omniscient, Omnipotent, and Omnipresent, etc. At this level of God, anything said is a decree that must stand just like whatever He says, declares, or speaks forth.

Since Jesus and God are the same in essence and are One, we know that all powers on earth and heaven are yielded unto Him. Therefore, our Lord Jesus would have His way in all matters of power and authority to bring them to existence. He was the One with God at the beginning; nothing was made without Him. Shifting focus away from the models of God and Christ, who occupy a class of their own, for the price that any man or woman or boy or girl has paid, a certain power and authority would be given to some, who would be able to operate in this realm. When we survey people who fall into this category truthfully, it could be said that a high-level concentration on God and devotion to Him were the trademarks to the degree that the mouths of those ones have become a vessel or an instrument in the hand of God to loose or bound on earth. The chronicles of such men are of enviable status, and they all proceeded to become spiritual Hall of Famers. From Moses to Joshua, to Eli, to Samuel, to Elijah, to Elisha, to Peter, to Paul, all of these in the biblical times have spoken forth, decreed, and declared words powered by an authority inside of them, which had resulted in amazing deeds, sometimes positive and sometimes doom, depending on what predicated the release of the decree of the declaration.

For instance, Eli the priest, having misjudged the action of Hannah, addressed her insultingly. But to the insult, Hannah responded respectfully, and this spurred the man of God to bless her: "Go in peace: and the God of Israel grant thee thy petition that thou hast asked of him" (1 Samuel 1:17, KJV). And that was it! The travail in prayers and fasting of almost two decades was sealed with a full-sentence declaration by Eli, which God granted. The following year, Hannah had her first child, Samuel.

King Ahaziah of Israel, angry with Elijah for his prophecy that he would not survive his disease, sent a band of fifty soldiers to arrest the man of God. The captain approached Elijah and called for him to come down. Then Elijah answered: "If I be a man of God, then let fire come down from heaven, and consume thee and thy fifty" (2 Kings 1:10a). That was it! Sanctioned! And there came down fire from heaven and licked the fifty-one soldiers.

Peter and John, at the hour of prayer, had gone to the temple to pray. There was a certain man, who was lame from his mother's womb, dropped at the gate for prospects of collecting alms. His intention was to see if they could give him money. Peter gazed upon him and said, "Silver and gold have I none; but such as I have give I thee: In the name of Jesus Christ of Nazareth rise up and walk" (Acts 3:6, KJV). That was it! He took him by the right hand and lifted him up, and his bones and ankle received strength. The man began to walk and leaped and praised God. The Lord honored the decree (Acts 3:1–26).

In Acts chapter 16, the young girl who was possessed by the spirit of divination encountered Paul. He turned to the spirit, "I command thee in the name of Jesus Christ to come out of her" (Acts 16:18, KJV). And we are told that immediately, the girl was delivered; the spirit left her.

These are a few of such great men who were totally sold to God to the point that they became a mouthpiece for the Lord that whatever they bound is bound or whatever they loose is loosed. Whatever was decreed or declared or spoken forth is done. It was a form of prayer instantaneously answered.

Today, you and I can still rise to this status of men who have proved right the words of Jesus: "Very truly I tell you, whoever believes in me will do the works I have been doing, and they will do even greater things than these, because I am going to the Father" (John 14:12, NIV). Greater opportunity is here to do great things and to declare and be done because we are to take over from where the Lord stopped at His return to the Father and at death for the New Testament fathers of faith.

To be square fit for this grace, we must exclusively exercise a great faith and walk right with God, being devoted and sanctified for Him. We cannot be flippant in our utterance. We must take steps to let the word of God dwell richly in us so that from the abundance of rich grace stored in us, the Holy Spirit could, from time to time, under appropriate and warranted circumstances, release power through the proclamations and declarations that come out of our mouths. The preparations on the ground would make our words prayers that heaven cannot but answer instantaneously with a resounding affirmation. There is much good and great work that God can and wants to do through us today.

3. ASK

Critics of spirituality throughout history have always attempted to cast aspersions on oblations that appear to disregard the ordinary practical pursuits of getting things done without God. Prayer, as a prime of example of that which provides solution to life questions without totally dependent on philosophy or ordinary actions of man, has offended the secularists of this age. Philip Yancey referenced such a view of the critics of prayer, who had seen it as an escapist way of dealing with problems.[27] The picture drawn for their sympathizers is that of a group of people who gather in a corner of life, send prayers to God, and thereafter lazily remain inactive, waiting for "manna" to fall from heaven. Charles Dickens, in one of his classics, actually drew that caricature of prayer through a character with a most appropriate name, Mr. Pecksniff. Saying grace before a bountiful meal, Pecksniff committed "all person who had nothing to eat to the care of providence, whose business (so said the grace, in effect) it clearly was to look after them."[28]

But Dickens cannot be right exclusively. Apostle James' epistle debunked this notion:

> *If a brother or sister be naked, and destitute of daily food,*
>
> *And one of you say unto them, Depart in peace, be ye warmed and filled; notwithstanding ye give them not those things which are needful to the body; what doth it profit?*
>
> *Even so faith, if it hath not works, is dead, being alone.*
>
> **James 2:15–17 (KJV)**

Believers active in prayer are far from the wrong notion, and the stereotypes created by the haters of spiritual things portrayed James. And those of us fervently given to prayers know better. No wonder Christ, in His uttermost ability to supply answers to ageless questions, offers teachings that square all complaints. He gave us a triplet form of prayers.

Yancey, in "Ask, Seek, and Knock," reveals the practical aspects involved in prayer, contrary to the thinking of prayer critics.[29] These three forms of prayer could relate in level of intensity, activities, and modalities. They are kind of related, though they are different. Jesus, our Lord, is the inventor of these three kinds of prayer. In Matthew 7:7 (KJV), the Lord said: "Ask, you shall receive; seek, you will find; knock and the door shall be opened to thee" (paraphrased). In a graduating format, they would show us how faith in prayer without work in prayer does not perfectly fit the original intent of the inventor of prayers.

The earlier verse continues: "For every one that asketh receiveth" (verse 8, KJV). Further up in scripture, James validated the words of Christ: "Yet you do not have because you do not ask" (James 4:2b, NKJV). Asking as a form of prayer reveals that if you have a need or desire, you need to ask God for it. In other words, you must express your want to your Father God. Of course, there is the underlying presupposition that all precautions and facilitators that aid and abet effectiveness of prayer are on the ground.

In essence, asking is the act of simply telling the

Lord, as in a prayer, that this is what my need (or want) is, and I really would love to have it. Perhaps the biggest lesson we learn from the origination of this prayer is that it is not all things that we need or are needed to make our lives complete that will automatically come to us nor be presented by our Father God. Sometimes, He relishes in seeing our understanding of the need, which can catapult us into asking for the filling in of the void. It is indicative of good partnership of life that God the Giver has given us to live for His glory and our personal fulfillment and joy.

Therefore, it is behooved upon us to learn to ask God for supply of our needs. It is an expression of dependency on Him.

4. SEEK

Seeking is a higher level of desperation or intensity in asking God for a thing. In seeking, movement is added to mere asking God for a request in a place of prayer.

Therefore, seeking brings practicality into our prayers. For instance, a man needs a job to earn a living so he can start making money. Perhaps he started by praying (and every child of God must begin the process of meeting a need by asking God in prayer) and has been praying for about a week or two. Then he receives a call from a friend that he just learned that a certain company or an establishment is hiring qualified people for certain positions. Immediately, our friend in need shifted gear into the mode of seeking, attempting to ask more questions about the employment—what needs to be done, the mode of applying, what is required at the interview, how to appear, what kind of questions to expect, etc. He could conduct research on the company's operation to broaden his knowledge of the company.

All these efforts (and much more) are the processes of seeking. Seeking refers to the general legworks that are preparatory to achieving the meeting of a need. It is part of the process of turning a verbal request, a wish, or a desire into a practical, concrete, and tangible supply. Seeking occupies those uncertain gaps between asking and receiving. God certainly designed and has used seeking to further purposes and answer prayers. Though history has recorded unusual answering of prayers that involve provision supply in the restricted place of prayer, and though some will still happen because God is unfathomably big and innovative, more often than not, there would always be that gap between asking and receiving from God that legworks will be the bane.

5. KNOCK

It is the most aggressive upper end of the process that begins with asking. We already know how seeking may need to follow the initiation of asking, but what we need to graduate to is the narrowing down of the varieties and pinpointing one or a few focal points that attention may now need to focus on.

Figuratively, choices have narrowed down to one avenue that has to be deeply explored. Usually, there will be the last barriers strong and sturdy, enough a challenge to just muster energy to deal with. It is the door! It has to be knocked traditionally unless it is your own place and you own a key to it. And so, knock, you must, says Jesus, before you enter into the place of fulfillment or one wealthy place.

Knocking process depicts amongst other reflections: "I won't take a 'no' for answer," and "I will do all that I needed to do." For the scripture enjoins all: When you have done all you can, stand. It denotes I must not leave any stone unturned, attitude as well as action. In this line, we are reminded of Jacob's encounter with the angel (Genesis 32:24). Something inside of the man who needed a destiny makeover really badly indicated that the stranger was the door leading to his life answer. This door has got to open, and he determined to knock it hard. And hard he did, and surely opened was the door. His life prayer got answered regardless of whether heaven was ready for him or not on that day. He determined for himself what one may have left for the other party to decide. This is wisdom: who else would favor you more than yourself? This is the mindset of anyone who will gainfully employ the recommended act of "knocking" to his benefit in the place of prayer.

The blind Bartimaeus encounter was another momentous example of what it is like to "bang" on the door. That Bartimaeus yearned that he could see would be an understatement; for anyone who had a brief experience of glued eyes for an hour would know that blindness is one of the diseases on earth that any man would love to sideline at all cost. The eye is the lamp of the body. To not see is an unquantifiable disadvantage. Having heard (but not able to witness) of many unbelievable miracles that Christ had performed, he was convinced that an opportunity with Jesus was definitely capable of turning his lifelong mourning into dancing.

And all he had for long wistfully fantasized came point-blank at him on this particular day unexpectedly: Jesus of Nazareth, the miracle-working Christ, was passing by. The more this sounded real, the greater his heart pounded that his time had come if he would seize the moment. And, of course, time was not a guaranteed ally. At every second that ticked, the harsh prospect was that his sight was ticking away unless he knocked the door. And he had to knock it hard. And indeed, he rolled up his sleeves and banged hard.

Even at the threat of intimidation of the flowing noise of the passerby crowd and of those who carefreely incited him to keep quiet and mellow down, he refused to back down and shouted: "Jesus, thou son of David, have mercy on me" (Mark 10:47b, KJV). That was him knocking the door really hard. Of course, Jesus is the door to the Father's Kingdom, where there is access to all things. Thanks to the Lord and His mercies, he received his sight (Mark 10:46).

Every child of God who is inhabited by the Holy Spirit is apt to identify those rare moments of life when what is at stake is the head of the snake and not the tail. In these momentous instances, the attitude and ensuing actions are reminiscent of the popular spiritual warfare song: "Today, Today, Today, Today, Jesus will answer me Today, Today, Today, Today, not tomorrow, The Lord has answered me, today, today."[30]

The woman with the issue of blood passed the alley. So did the malefactor nailed to a cross at the right side of Christ at Calvary (Luke 8:43, 23:32). These and many more would not spare the door when it is point-blank—the answer to the prayer was lifelong and eternal in some cases.

6. OBEDIENCE TO GOD AND HIS WORDS

Another typology of prayer is obedience to God. Fundamentally, every word of God ever spoken has been directed to men for information and instruction. Therefore, most of what we know about God, we access through what He says in His Word: the compilation of His words called the Bible or scripture (though sometimes, those who are endowed with extra spiritual gifts could hear/receive words that may be unilaterally and privately applied).

Paul, under inspiration, opened our minds to the unquantifiable benefit of the Word of God. In 2 Timothy 3:16, we are informed that the word of God is useful for shaping our lives in a solid form, rebuking, corrective to the point where a Christian could live a very successful and purposeful life. In the end, he becomes well-armed and equipped to become the best person that God had intended him to be at creation. These two verses convincingly prove that step-by-step walking of life's activities is already spelled for us by God in His Word. If we take them to heart and live by them, i.e., if we obediently follow God's instructions, we mature to the success and fulfillment that God originally intended.

There is a powerful correlation between obedience and prayer. Mathematically, we can deduce that both are mutually exclusive, as in an equation of success or blessing. Jesus postulates: "If ye abide in me and my words abide in you, ye shall ask what ye will [pray], and it shall be done unto you" (John 15:7, KJV). In other words, "For your prayers to be fully answered, you must be close to Me, honor My words, and do them." No wonder Samuel told Saul the king, "Behold, to obey is better than sacrifice, and to hearken than the fat of rams" (1 Samuel 15:22b, KJV). Previously in the earlier part of the exchange, it had been made known that God is not delighted in burnt offerings and the obvious running around helter-skelter of people than in simply doing whatever the Lord wants us to do.

Our God is simply saying, "Receive My words, follow My instructions to letter, and you will be universally blessed." In other words, where there is obedience, formal prayer is less needed because the majority of blessings are automatic derivatives of doing what God instructs men to do.

In Hebrews 11:6, the word of God is expressed: Without faith, it is impossible to please the Lord, for all who will approach God must first believe that He is and that He is a rewarder of all that diligently seek Him. To diligently seek Him is to follow after Him. To follow after Him is to know Him, do all He commands, and serve Him. Rewards are blessings we partly receive for our efforts that are underwritten by pleasing and obeying the Lord.

The survey of the Israelites' deliverance and their eventual ferrying across the waters and desert to the Promised Land really credentials the power of obeying God as a means of achieving big. It also underscores the goodness and anticipation of God concerning our success. He had plans and purposes for us, which His pleasure is that we accomplish them on record time to His glory and to our joy and satisfaction (cf: Jeremiah 29:11). The only instances when the Israelites throughout their journey had to pray were those occasions following steering away from His instructions and times of rebellion against Him. Ordinarily, provisions were coming, and generally, God was leading by way of clouds by day, fire by night, and instructions through Moses and later Joshua, who succeeded him.

Hear some of what the Lord told His people:

> *Therefore thou shall love the LORD thy God, and keep his charge, and his statutes, and his judgments, and his commandments, alway. Therefore ye shall keep all the commandments*

which I command you this day, that ye may be
strong, and go in to possess the land, whither
ye go to possess it...

Deuteronomy 11:1, 8 (KJV)

"And it shall come to pass, if thou shall hearken diligently unto the voice of the LORD...all these blessings...." (Deuteronomy 28:1–2a, KJV)

Here the message is abundantly clear: "Obey Me, follow My instructions; you will be exceptionally blessed and established to the point that 'all people of the earth shall see that thou art called by [My name] the name of the Lord; and they shall be afraid of thee'" (Deuteronomy 28:10, KJV). Even beyond blessing, we will be protected and secured. It will be challenging to calculate the volume of (how much) prayers that will accomplish these vast blessings and benefits. I want to subscribe to the fact that God never intended that a life of prayers exclusively would substitute for obeying His words. Prayer is meant to deliver where genuine challenges appear, mostly because of our dutifulness and loyalty to God. Later on, we will see how disobedience will actually trump (truncate) prayers.

7. Dwelling in God

To dwell in God is to stay with Him within the confines of His safe arms. To everyone who truly belongs to God, there is a place of safety and success carved for him. Each of us is a part of the whole body. We have a "place" and "neighbors" that link with us and, ultimately, link with the "head," Jesus Christ, we all fit well together and can do very well according to the original plan of God (1 Corinthians chapter 12). Jesus expresses it thus,

> *Abide in me and I in you. As the branch cannot bear fruit of itself, except it abide in the vine; no more can ye, except ye abide in me. I am the vine, ye are the branches: He that abideth in me, and I in him, the same bringeth forth much fruit: for without me ye can do nothing.*
>
> **John 15:4–5 (KJV)**

We are clearly told to be very fruitful (to be successful), we must, as a part, be in the Lord: attached to Him, dwell in Him, and be connected to Him for continuous nutrient supply and productivity potential. With respect to wealth, the word of God reminds us that not much can be successfully garnered by our own hands and strength, but instead, we must know that the power to get wealth is only endowed of God that He may establish His covenant He *swore* unto our fathers, as it is this day (Deuteronomy 8:18). In other words, God reminds us that it is in connecting with Him in close fellowship that a "special power" or acumen to make wealth can be obtained.

To have wealth and enjoy peace can only be possible when in God you are dwelling, and you contact your success. There are those who are "wealthy" or "successful" but don't have peace, and their lives are projected sorrowful because their end is sour. Like the rich described by Jesus, their getting to heaven is nothing more than a mirage. But come to think of it, Jesus cautions, "What shall it profit a man, if he shall gain the whole world, and lose his own soul?" (Mark 8:36, KJV)

But for those who choose to live in God, they receive a kind of blessing that is not threatened by sorrows. This is because real blessings are given to those who stay in God.

For security in life, the psalmist emphasizes the importance of dwelling in God: "He that dwelleth in the secret place of the most High shall abide under the shadow of the Almighty" (Psalm 91:1, KJV). He was sure no place of being safe is better than the confines of God.

Solomon also echoes the powerful sentiment: "The name of the LORD is a strong tower; The righteous run to it and are safe" (Proverbs 18:10, NKJV). And for as long as they stay in this place of refuge, no evil can overcome them. "The LORD is my shepherd; I shall not want" (Psalm 23:1, KJV), confidently sang David, the man who knows how to live in God and trust Him practically. Nothing ensures a better-blessed life than staying under the canopy that God had provided for His children, like prayers answered before it was even offered. That is heaven on earth!

Perhaps the most encompassing illustration and emphatic lesson on this topic are offered by the popular narrative of Christ titled "The Prodigal Son." Imagine for a moment how blessed and fulfilled the young man was before he even knew how to spell his own name. Born into sufficiency in all ramifications, and that is the picture for all men, especially all who are born again (John chapter 3) and who have received the Lord as Savior and so obtained the power to become the children of God (John 1:12). The beauty of such a life is: For as long as you stay inside, you are fully fulfilled in all matters of life, now and in eternity. But as the case was with the prodigal son, he walked out of the radius of the long hands of the Father (Lord), stepping out of the safety zone and dropping off the everlasting arms. When this happens to anyone, no amount of prayers will suffice, but a better timely and equipped prayer, which is "returning to dwell in God," as the prodigal son eventually did.

8. PRAYING IN THE SPIRIT

This terminology is given to a form of prayer offered by the spirit of the Lord, allocated a comfort zone in our hearts. This is a prayer that is Spirit-initiated.

As a genuine believer, the spirit of the Lord, the Holy Spirit, comes into our hearts the moment we truly commit our lives to God, i.e., when we become born again. As we seek the Lord more in His words, devotion, and fellowship with others in the body (church) setting, the Holy Spirit in us also begins to develop "muscles" to the point of manifestation—that is, revealing His power and work in us. One of manifestation of the spirit is praying to the Father God on our behalf.

The Holy Spirit knows the mind of God because He is the spirit of God. Because of this powerful advantage—knowing the Father and His children's minds simultaneously—He is a helper to us (John chapter 14). From time to time, He voluntarily proceeds to pray for us knowing the perfect will of God for us. No prayer is better offered than the one that matches the perfect will of God for us. Sometimes, it may come as "tongues" in our private prayer time for those endowed with that manifestation of the Spirit (1 Corinthians 12:10). For some others, His intercessions come as groaning too profound to be uttered in words that can be clearly articulated (Romans 8:26). Either way, the One who answers prayers, our Father God, understands, and He would hear and answer both (1 Peter 3:12).

The bottom line is that this kind of prayer must not be absent in our lives, for they are very effective because it is often formulated and offered by the third person of the Trinity, who coincidentally is the representative of God in our lives, who has been posted in us as the Helper, Teacher, and Comforter. Because of His omniscient nature, His prayer for us is akin to the striking of the bull's eye. These are adequate content and perfectly uttered prayers that cannot escape God's hearing. In the circle of prayer, the Holy Ghost cannot be beaten. His intercessions for us will always make all things work for good for all who are God's children (verse 28).

For a believer to enjoy this benefit from time to time,

you must endeavor to be filled with the Spirit. How to be filled? Study and meditate on the Word of God, fellowship with God and His people as much as you can, and think about things that are virtuous, praiseworthy, godly, and spiritual. These and some more in the line of godliness are the ingredients that enhance the infilling and building of spiritual muscles that often lead to the spirit of God kicking into intercession mode for His residence. For we are temples of the Holy Spirit.

9. AGREEMENT

One form of prayer is agreement with someone on a matter. Agreeing with another person concerning an issue could bring it to existence.

Jesus Christ laid this down when He said, "If two of you shall agree on earth as touching any thing that they shall ask [desire], it shall be done for them of my Father which is in heaven" (Matthew 18:19, KJV). This is often alluded to regarding what a great thing can be accomplished, just like a hard-labored prayer answered when there is agreement between two people, especially husband and wife. Though spouses readily come to mind, the power here is not restricted to couples. Brothers, friends, and even enemies who, for a moment, agree, can usually accomplish a goal. Such was the case with Herod and Pilate when Jesus was on trial to be condemned to die. We were intimated that Pilate and Herod were antagonists before this day, but the cause of Jesus pitched them on the same side. Eventually and coincidentally, the big goal of taking Jesus out was accomplished. If enemies in temporary sync could do profoundly, how much more those who are well related on good grounds and godly causes?

In verse 20 of Matthew chapter 18 (KJV), Jesus continued, "Where two or three [or more] are gathered together in my name, there am I in the midst of them." This extension is an added grace that, for settings like familiars, churches, associations, states, nations, etc., if all can simply agree on a point or project, it will get accomplished.

Therefore, highlighted is the power of agreement that it is a prayer auto-answered. The historical account of the Tower of Babel is a case point that is, most persuasively, admissible on this platform. These were people not inspired by God but by their own ego and prowess, who chose to rise up and reach God where He was by simply erecting a tower that would take them to such a height harboring the beautiful abode of God.

Simple. They started to build. They were united and unanimously agreed to do it. They got God's attention by the imminent success of the venture. And since their venture was not according to God's will, they had to be stopped by an injection of a neutralizing ingredient to what was working for them. God confused their tongues to castrate the power of unity they were harnessing. Because they could not agree due to lack of mutual understanding, the project was abandoned (Genesis 11:1–9).

Get a person with you or a group of people with you and come to a solid agreement. You don't necessarily need a forty-day fasting or sporadic night vigils. What you intend to do will get done if the agreement price can be afforded.

Just as agreement in prayer is essential, I submit that on a special terrain, simple agreement will get a job done when all come together to do their own part. Interestingly, conventional wisdom has sadly revealed that when a group of people comes together, even church people inclusive, more prayers are needed for agreement than are needed to directly seek God's approval. How ironical!

CHAPTER 6:

PECULIARITIES OF PRAYERS

Success is never accidental. The successful in all ventures have always identified the codes that are diligently unraveled en route to blossoming in the chosen undertaking. So it is with a crack at prayer. Identifying and appealing to prayer's unique attributes have always manufactured a smiling face out of the altar of mercy and grace.

The peculiarities of prayers are those attributes that are unique about them; those make a prayer to be in a class of its own, whereby to especially enjoy it qualitatively, one must be able to connect with and tap the benefits of that uniqueness. Connecting with and tapping into that uniqueness is like tuning into a radio or a television frequency. Whenever that is achieved, a radio station sounds clearly; in case of a television, it gives a succinct, clear picture.

1. TIME OF PRAYER

Some special, good, and effective prayers do have a time factor that marks them into a special class. Though in an angle, we are taught to pray without ceasing (1 Thessalonians 5:17); yet, we must understand that there are some specially commissioned assignments that must get completed at some specific times. Men of God and good intercessors have learned to flow in these special times for purposes of efficiency of prayer.

In Acts chapter 3, we read the account of how Peter and John, on this particular day, rose up to go to the temple at the time of prayer. I tagged the day "particular" because of the special result of prayer experienced on that day. It was for them a formed habit and a determination to be in the temple on such hours to pray. The reality of the strong power that greeted that prayer probably had a lot to do with the determination, purposefulness, focus, and the spiritual zeal with which the act was displayed.

Our Lord Jesus gave us the confidence when He said that whenever two or three (or more) are gathered together in His name, He will be present (Matthew 18:20). This strongly indicated that when a time is zeroed on for prayer ahead of time, Jesus—the prayer answerer—is alerted, and so big things can legitimately be expected.

For instance, the psalmist gave us something to seriously consider when out of divine wisdom, He said,

"My Father and God, early in the morning will I seek thee" (paraphrased) (Psalm 63:1, KJV). In this utterance, two points stand out: "Early" is a word denoting the element of time and timing. "Early" means coming earlier than other times. There are times, but surely, "early" comes before the regular and normal time and, for sure, before late time.

Secondly, "seek thee" means going after God in prayers. Therefore, by combining the two points, the psalmist is saying that the early part of our daily time, when we are still fresh, full of vitality, not yet polluted or saddled with many thoughts and self-plans for the day that is breaking, is obviously a wisely preferred time for prayers that will achieve more or get more results. Realistically, a time when better results are assured can be tagged "the time of." Laying bigger weight to this point was the great father of faith John Bunyan. He was quoted as saying, "He who runs from God in the morning will scarcely find Him the rest of the day."[31] In other words, he is saying, "To really be sure that your prayer will be answered, call upon the Lord early (in the morning or any other time peculiarly preeminent to you)." Make the necessary sacrifice to call upon the Lord at this "money" time. It was Prophet Isaiah who had earlier on prophesied it aloud and clearly: "Seek the LORD while He may be found. Call upon Him while He is near" (Isaiah 55:6, NKJV). The availability of God, for sure, is a function of time, amongst other variables.

Another giant of prayer, E. M. Bounds, echoed the same sentiment but using different words: "The men who have done the most for God in this world have been early on their knees." (I believe he had David in mind.) He continued,

> *He who fritters away the early morning, its opportunity and freshness, in other pursuits than seeking God will make poor headway seeking Him the rest of the day. If God is not first in our thoughts and efforts in the morning, He will be in the last place the remainder of the day.*[32]

In other words, "early" is a precise determinant of how we can expect God to be prominent in our full day's affairs. For believers who depend solely on the power and grace of God to be able to accomplish and do all things (Philippians 4:13), this becomes a very big deal.

There is also the preciseness of time. Solomon opened our eyes and minds to how certain events and accomplishments in our lives are preordained and pre-timed. In Ecclesiastes chapter 3, we are intimated with a helpful divine principle:

> *To every thing there is a season, and a time to every purpose under the heaven: a time to be born, a time to plant.... a time to heal...a time to build up, a time to laugh...a time to dance...a time to embrace, a time to keep silence, a time to speak, a time to love...a time of peace...*

> **Ecclesiastes 3:1–8 (KJV)**

This passage shared with us a chronicle of the ordained times for both positive and negative events. Paying attention helps us to know how to employ prayer at crucial times to lock in blessings and the good and fence off the negatives and undesirables. How expeditiously a good accomplishment would be realized, which has been ordained and jumpstarted by a timely prayer.

Nothing is more successful than a life propelled by the Holy Spirit to pray pre-ordained accomplishments into reality. There is nothing easier and better accomplished than that which God has already finished in the spirit realm. Put in a very simple, clear format: when prayers are offered in respect of a matter that is destined to run at the time, such prayers have enjoyed the precision timing that makes them very effective. A spirit-led man will not play with the benefits of time of prayer. It is a bull's eyes striking mechanism with a precision and effectiveness that is second to none.

We are reminded of more momentous examples of people in biblical history who drew their miracles through the power of the time of supplication. Blind Bartimaeus had Jesus of Nazareth at a very close range. Something inside of him pinched him forcefully, alerting him that his chance of a lifetime—his sight was passing by. His sight was in the hand of the miracle worker, and every split second of delay would be eternally disastrous. So, he shouted and screamed: "Jesus of Nazareth, have mercy on me!" Even at the abject discouragement and from those nearby who obviously did not obtain the revelation he got. He disregarded their antic, and in the mannerism of knocking, he literally banged on the door until Jesus could no longer ignore his voice. That very minute, heaven smiled on him—his prayer was instantaneously answered. That was his day, his hour, his minute, and his second! His sight was forever restored.

Every true believer who aspires to maximize God's input in the affairs of their lives must seek the prompting of the Holy Ghost to drive us to our knees or instigate us to rise up our holy hands in supplications to the Lord at "the times of prayers." This we must graciously seek.

2. PLACE OF PRAYER

Again, though certain principle teaches that a group of people in the unity of their spirit can command the presence of Christ and, for their benefit, turn on an atmosphere of favor in prayers, we also know convincingly that God Himself can ordain places where, if any man could get to those spaces, God will move on his behalf. There are places designated as places where prayers are answered most effectively.

A. **A place where people gather in the name of Christ.** Where two or three are gathered in the name of Christ, He would be there to answer their bidding in prayer. That is a given (Matthew 18:20, ibid)! We, therefore, know that the gathering of the righteous in a particular place will usher in God's gracious and favorable response to prayers.

In the Upper Room, about 120 righteous, obedient followers of the ascended Christ came under one roof in unity. God responded with myriads of miracles in Acts chapter 2. The Upper Room became a place of prayer.

B. **The location of a pure-hearted man.** Even a man with a pure heart will turn his location to a place of prayer—where God answers the prayer of His own man. The psalmist declared: "Who shall ascend unto the hill of the LORD? He that hath clean hands, and a pure heart; who hath not lifted his soul unto vanity, nor sworn deceitfully. He shall receive the blessing from the Lord and righteousness from the God of his salvation" (Psalm 24:3a–4, KJV). There are places where the favors of God are ripe. One must go up there: the arena of answered prayers.

C. **A place of prayer designated by God Himself.** When the temple of David was completed, and Solomon led dedication offering to the Lord, the Lord Himself spoke and designated that temple a place where He could not refuse His people whenever they came with a request. Hear what God says, "I have heard thy prayer, and have chosen this place to myself for an house of sacrifice. If I shut up heaven that there be no rain, or if I command the locusts to devour the land, or if I send pestilence among my people; if my people, which are called by my name, shall humble themselves, and pray, and seek my face, and turn from their wicked ways; then will I hear from heaven, and will forgive their sin, and will heal their land. Now my eyes shall be open, and mine ears attent unto the prayer that is made in this place. For now have I chosen and sanctified this house, that my name may be there for ever: and mine eyes and mine heart shall be there perpetually" (2 Chronicles 7:12b–16, KJV).

This was a direct response to the dedication prayers, richly worded and voluminously loaded for the Lord to grant. And indeed, the Lord granted his prayers and designated that temple a place where God, even in anger, will cool off and, in pleasantness, will magnanimously bless His people.

For God's people, that was the right place to seek God's face. It was also the best time to have God as a father. Convincingly, the eyes of the Lord were upon them, and His ears were graciously open unto their requests (see 1 Peter 3:12).

D. **Solitary places.** A good survey of the ministerial operations of Jesus revealed that He was often pursued by restless people. The very moment people realized that He was capable of performing miracles, they thronged after Him for what they could get from Him. No wonder when He felt the urge or the necessity to pray, He would cross over into a place or those places where the hustle and bustle of the seekers would be minimized, and He could be in a solitary situation that is akin to facilitate concentration before the Lord (Matthew

14:23). So, we know that not every place is conducive to prayer that would be effective and powerful.

This recognition we must need to apply for our wisdom. In our world of today, we do experience partly what Jesus was experiencing in this realm. We are in the middle of a fast-moving world where our whole being is involved in a motion that could be hardly resisted. Wim Malgo, writing about the need to seek a quiet place of refuge for effective prayer, commented about how Jesus, a great Man of prayer, was pursued by restless people. He went further to observe how (also) "we are today surrounded by rushing nervous people."[33] Indeed, today, we are bombarded by family, work, association, children, dreams, sports, and even sometimes church activities. The awareness of these fast-tempo elements involving us also confronts us with the necessity of deliberately seeking antithetical situations better suited for fellowshipping with God one-on-one in prayer. The psalmist relevantly muttered: "Be still, and know that I am God: I will be exalted among the heathen, I will be exalted in the earth" (Psalm 46:10, KJV). Sometimes, life-giving and powerful prayers are manufactured in places of solitude (see 1 Kings 17:17–24; Matthew 6:6). We must adapt to emulate Jesus, who is reputable for doing that to His spiritual advantage (ibid.).

3. FREQUENCY OF PRAYER

Another peculiarity of prayer is the frequency factor. How often do you offer the same prayer? Getting the right answer could be the *depuzzling* that will ice the cake for a man seeking God's favor in prayer.

Though it is not every time that a prayer point would need to be offered, there are some prayers that represent them is the puzzle that a prayer warrior needs to solve before he would receive the blessing.

Jesus told the comparative narrative of two people who went to pray. One, the Pharisee was fully wording his prayers with every point that will get God's attention, but the publican was really low-key and expressed himself humbly before God with barely one full sentence of prayer: "Be merciful unto me a sinner!" Jesus concluded that the publican left God's presence, a man whose prayer was answered while the Pharisee went away condemned (Luke 18:9–16).

But in contrast, read the story of the fearless judge and the importunate widow (Luke 18:1–8). The helpless woman's prayer power was in her persistence. She refused intimidation and would not accept a "no" for an answer. She knocked hard and sought and asked. She reordered the modus operandi in a grand slam style. Her persistence was the key.

Therefore, we must acknowledge that there are prayers that would only be effective when the right frequency is struck. That is the peculiarity that when unearthed, a man can walk away from the presence of the Lord bigger than he may ever imagine.

Paul encourages believers to always pray, i.e., without ceasing (1 Thessalonians 5:17). Isaiah spoke prophetically about the effectiveness of staying in God's presence. "They that wait upon the LORD shall renew their strength...." (Isaiah 40:31a, KJV)

In other words, there are times and prayer preoccupations that must keep our knees deep down in God's periphery, and this we must do in order that our prayer may be fully utilized. Prophet Daniel entered a long fasting to deal with a cause that was huge to him. Even though, as God would later reveal, his prayers had been approved since the first day, Angel Gabriel was hindered from delivering the answer to Daniel. So, he continued the fasting until the twenty-first day of the month when God recognized the travail of Daniel. *This guy, by now, should be enjoying the reward of his prayers*, God thought, and so Angel Michael was dispatched to rescue the blessing and delivered it to him (Daniel chapter 10).

The point was, no backing down in prayers was the strength of this supplication. Daniel took up the challenge, and the Lord answered.

4. DEPENDENCY

It is not a slam dunk that every prayer reveals total dependence on God. Sometimes, people pray with the mindset that they just have to pray because it is good to pray, or, as children of God, we ought to pray. A lot of times, prayers are said just for the sake of saying so we may feel good that we have done one of those essential and important oblations of a real believer.

But in practical reality, there are times when our prayers essentially lean totally on God. Such a time highlights the uniqueness of prayer. In such situations, we discover the peculiarity that is exclusively attached to prayer as a mode of getting God on our side to get things done.

Prophet Isaiah draws us into such moments and situations in one of his writing:

> *For the Lord GOD will help me; therefore shall I not be confounded: therefore have I set my face like a flint, and I know that I shall not be ashamed. Behold, the Lord GOD will help me... Who is among you that feareth the LORD, that obeyeth the voice of his servant [...] let him trust in the name of the LORD, and stay upon his God.*
>
> **Isaiah 50:7, 9a–10 (KJV)**

There is the time and occasion when you know that if the Lord does not come to your aid, you are cooked. Prayers on such occasion are padded with total dependency. Faces are set like a flint to the only One who must help. Such prayers in such moods are powerfully effective.

The psalmist says, "I will lift up mine eyes unto the hills, from whence cometh my help. My help cometh from the LORD, which made heaven and earth" (Psalm 121:1–2, KJV). This was said in one of those seasons when the enemies were determined to take him out. A price tag was pinned on his head. But ironically, he struck an accord with dependency element of prayer. He impressed upon the Lord that there was no other place for him to go but Him. He expressed heartily that the name of the Lord was his only tower of refuge, and as the righteous of all ages had found safety, he, too, would.

In another place (Psalm 27), he exclaimed, "The LORD is my light and my salvation; whom shall I fear? The LORD is the strength of my life; of whom shall I be afraid?" (Psalm 27:1, KJV) This means that the Lord is the guide of his steps in life and the assurance of his security as he proceeds. He continued: "When the wicked, even mine enemies and my foes, came upon me to eat up my flesh, they stumbled and fell. Though an host should encamp against me… One thing I've desired of the Lord… for in the time of trouble…" (Psalm 27:2–5, KJV) Expressed without reservation is the total reliance and dependency upon the Lord. The enemies and foes, no matter how strong they look, must go down—when the Lord arises, all His enemies must dissipate; they must melt like wax before a great heat, and like smoke must be diffused before a wind (Psalm 68:1–2).

But the one who had hinged his unalloyed dependence on God will rejoice and be glad because God will surely come through in this atmosphere.

CHAPTER 7:

THE POWER INGREDIENTS OF PRAYER

*Prayerless Christians are powerless.
Endeavor to pray ceaselessly, and so shall
the ceaseless power acquired carry you
through a season of ceaseless Satanic
attack.*

Apostle James opened our eyes in his epistle as to why it is very important for a prayer to be powerful. A powerful prayer is the one that is effective and availing. When it is effective and availing, obviously, it has gotten the job done. Such an enviable label on prayer is after the fact of its success. I believe any serious prayer warrior, or anyone who cares to pray at all, yearns for the prayer to work, to accomplish the purpose for which the prayer is being offered.

He writes:

> *Is any of you in trouble? He should pray. Is anyone happy... And the prayer offered in faith will make the sick person well; the Lord will raise him up... The prayer of a righteous man is powerful and effective... Elijah was a man just like us. He prayed earnestly that it would not rain...*

James 5:13–17 (NIV)

From the words of James, certain elements appear to sustain the fabric of a powerful prayer. Such include prayer offered in faith (NIV), prayer of faith (KJV), prayer of the righteous man (NIV or KJV), sins confessed, and sins forgiven.

1. **Prayer of faith.** It is prayer offered by a man who believes in the Lord implicitly and who is confident that God can and has the capacity to answer prayers. Knowing and being internally convinced that God is omnipotent and unlimited in the ability to do things is power to the prayer. A man of faith is convinced that with God, all things are possible (Mark 9:23). With such a mindset, prayers offered are powerful and effective. Without faith, it is impossible to please the Lord. Those who will approach God and be blessed must believe in Him totally and that He is a rewarder of those who diligently seek Him (Hebrews 11:6). Those are people of faith, an ingredient of prayer power.

2. **Righteousness.** Righteousness is being right with God. The righteous are those who, through the saving blood and powers of Jesus, are redeemed for God and who live according to His dictates. The righteousness of a child of God is power to his prayers. The righteous calls on to God, and He answers him (Psalm 34:17). The Lord will not withhold anything good from those who are walking uprightly before God (Psalm 84:11). Who shall ascend on to the hills of the Lord? Only those with clean hands and a pure heart (Psalm 24:3). These are the righteous of God. As a father cannot give stone to his child who asks for bread or give serpent to him that asks for fish, so God cannot turn His eyes away or withdraw a benevolent hand from His child who is upright (Matthew 7:9–10). He loves His children.

3. **Sins confessed.** David exclaimed, "If I regard iniquity in my heart, the Lord will not hear me" (Psalm 66:18, KJV). God, we are told, does not answer the prayers of sinners (John 9:31). Their prayer is an abomination to Him (Proverbs 28:7). Sin will becloud prayers and so diminish their power and efficacy. But when a person opens his life to the Lord and confesses his sins, we are told that God is merciful and just to forgive and to cleanse us from all of our unrighteousness. He can't turn away a sinner who is willing to repent. Coming bare before the Lord is an empowerment to the prayer because the scripture reveals: "He who covers his sins will not prosper" (Proverbs

28:13, NKJV). It is a key to the power of prayer that sins are confessed and willingness to repent is laid bare. In so doing, the blood of Jesus is being put to work, which is instrumental to maximizing the sacrifice of our Savior on the cross. To this, the Lord is pleased.

4. **Forgiveness of sins.** Those who confess their sins and are willing to come clean are forgiven of the Lord, and such has their prayer coated with power.

The Lord, responding to the dedication prayer of Solomon, proceeded to declare: "If my people, which are called by my name, shall humble themselves, and pray, and seek my face, and turn from their wicked ways; then will I hear from heaven, and will forgive their sin, and will heal their land" (2 Chronicles 7:14, KJV).

Sin is a hindrance to prayer. Sins must be cleared for the prayer of the righteous to be powerful. "For the wages of sin is death; but the gift of God is eternal life through Jesus Christ our Lord" (Romans 6:23, KJV). Uncleared and unforgiven sins can only result in calamity and, ultimately, death. This is an end that does not tally with what prayer is built to achieve. Ability to pray really is a gift of God. Endowments from God that manifest as spiritual gifts are given to us to profit (1 Corinthians 12:7). Since prayer is sought to release God's grace, help, and, ultimately, life of abundance, no wonder sin is a deterrent. Sin must not be allowed in the place of prayer because it will work to truncate the goals set forth. To maximally enjoy the benefits of prayer, sins that will erode its power must be appropriately dealt with. Sins in the life of a believer are meant to be repented of and turned away. This is the plat we reach to earn the forgiveness of God.

Other power ingredients of prayer include:

5. **Persistency.** Luke chapter 18 starts by introducing the lesson of that day taught by Jesus: "And he *spake*[2] a parable unto them to this end, that men ought always to pray, and not to faint" (verse 1, KJV). New International Version (NIV) rendition is simpler: "Then Jesus told his disciples a parable to show them that they should always pray and not give up." In the parable, a troubled woman saw the judge as the man with power who could help her clear her issues. She pressed against the initial objection of the benefactor. Eventually, her persistence broke the back of the unwillingness of the big man (verse 1 to 7). Seeing that the importunate widow was not going to let off and fearing that the pressure would have no end, he acquiesced to her request.

Jesus the Master uses this to teach us persistency at the place of prayer when we have not obtained the answer. For as long and often, we must dig in our knees in prayer.

In our modern-day gospel churches, we have an acronym for this element of power in prayer:

---

2 Hereinafter, emphasis added.

PUSH—"**P**ray **U**ntil **S**omething **H**appens."[34] Of course, those of us given to incessant prayers know that when prayers begin to pour, some things must happen, and trust me, to the ones who pray, bad things will not happen ultimately. Only good and better things are bound to occur! The thoughts of the legendary woman of prayer, Mary Warburton Booth, fit perfectly here: "Depend upon it, if you are bent on prayer, the devil will not leave you alone. He will molest you. What he minds and opposes steadily is the prayer that prays until it is prayed through, assured of the answer."[35] She is very right. The arch enemy would not mind you doing prayers that bring no answer, but he is very ready to oppose you when you are determined to not come up empty. Good thing: Our determined persistence will always top his opposition no matter how skillful it is because we are backed by the word, which encourages us to "resist the devil, and he will flee from you" (James 4:7b, KJV).

Philip Yancey, in his book *Prayer: Does It Make a Difference?* quoted E. M Bounds (author of eight books on prayer) of words that are perfect for our stand here: "Prayer in its highest form and grandest success assume the attitude of a wrestler with God."[36] Yancey continued his own equally relevant thought: "Our no-holds-barred outbursts hardly threaten God, and sometimes they even seem to change God. As the touch on Jacob's hip socket proved, God could have ended the match at any point during that long night in the desert, instead the elusive lingered, as eager to be held as Jacob was to hold."[37] This sounds like an attribute of a hard-core Pentecostal prayer warrior. In the circles of prayers, strange things had always happened with this attitude. They are always testimonies of inductive manifestations.

In 1979, my friend's wife's dad rose up in the mortuary after his daughter refused to stop praying that her dad could not just leave the earth like that without conversing with her. After about eight hours of prayer, the father woke up and spoke with her before lying down finally!

Sometimes, our persistence in the place of prayer may have to be wordless, expressionless, and nonverbal, like the psalmist when he expressed: "I will lift up mine eyes unto the hills, from whence cometh my help. My help cometh from the LORD, which made heaven and earth" (Psalm 121:1–2, KJV). Maybe you've got to the extreme end, and no words could come out (ibid.). Everything seems to have been exhausted; like David, you can go beyond wordiness in prayer and fix your gaze on God just as the crippled man of the Beautiful Gate fastened his eyes on Peter and John. Just as the man went home with his miracle, I pray that you will end your day with the graphic touch of the divine upon your life in the name of Jesus! Don't give up until the Lord says yes to your asking.

6. **Fasting.** Fasting is to prayer what the iron rods are to a mere mixture of water, sand, gravel, and

cement. Just as the resultant compound from the latter, prayer, when combined with fasting, becomes concrete that can sustain lots and lots of building weights, so in a similar fashion, prayers accompanied with fasting becomes so potent that it brings unbelievable and amazing results, sometimes called miracles.

In Mark chapter 9, a boy possessed and fully controlled by a demon was brought by his father to Jesus having heard about His ability to perform miracles—thousands of people have been fed not just on one occasion, the deaf ears have opened up, a deaf-mute has been healed, woman with the issue blood for twelve years had been healed, a tomb-inhabited demoniac had been delivered and set free, and many of various diseases have been healed, etc. (see Mark chapters 3 to 8). According to the man, his boy had been totally overwhelmed by this demon, which, in addition to muting him, would occasionally engulf him. Whenever this occurred, he would floor him, causing him to foam, gnashing his teeth, and pine away (verses 17 to 18). Compassionate and moved, Jesus rebuked the foul spirit commanding him to come out and never enter back. On hearing the voice of Jesus, the spirit screamed and rent the boy sore and came out of him, leaving the boy lifeless (because he had full charge upon his body). Jesus then, seeing that the crowd had concluded him for dead, moved forward and raised the body up, and his life was resorted (verses 25 to 27). This miracle awed the large crowd, including His disciples.

The account continued that when Jesus and His disciples got back into the privacy of the house, they asked the Master: "Why could we not cast the demon out like you did?" And Jesus answered: "This kind can come forth by nothing but by prayer and fasting." This was a huge spiritual secret unveiled.

From whence we know that beating up on the flesh of man would empower the Spirit more, which is exactly what transpires when fasting occurs, whereby the body is denied strength due to non supply of food, albeit willingly. The miraculous and the amazing can only be accomplished and performed in the power and operation of the Spirit, often precipitated through powerful and availing prayers. Andre Murray, one of such men given to powerful prayers, discovered this secret formula when he said, "Prayer is far-reaching out after the unseen; fasting is letting go of all that is seen and temporal. Fasting helps express, deepen, and confirm the resolution that we are ready to sacrifice anything, even ourselves, to attain what we seek for the Kingdom of God."[38] I believe the soul of the secret behind fasting is the sacrifice of the denial of that which is most desired, in order to receive what is greater in value and essence. In his powerful faith classic written over a century ago, A. A. Allen, a man whose ministry was distinctive for the moves of the Holy Spirit, believed very strongly that fasting is an important part of self-denial. He continued in his remarks that the desire for food—the richest, tastiest, and best—is one of the strongest desires of self. It was for food that Esau sold his birthright. It was to physical hunger—the desire for food that Satan directed the first in a series of temptations to Christ in the wilderness.[39] No wonder Jesus fasted for forty days, denied Himself food and drink, but at the end was awarded the miracle of soundly beating the devil (Matthew 4:1–11).

Paul, the great apostle that many of us would love to be like in terms of the grace upon his life, was no stranger to this principle. He told us that often he was in watching, in hunger and thirst, in fasting... (2 Corinthians 11:27) No wonder miracles, signs, and wonders were rife in his ministry.

Many of the twenty-first century great men of God, whom God used in some profound and incredible ways, were men who were not only strong in prayer but resilient in fasting. Apostle Joseph Ayodele Babalola, the founder of CAC Worldwide, blazed the landscape of Nigeria with jaw-breaking miracles at the commencement of his ministry and the church in 1930. The miraculous was bold in the history of Christianity in Nigeria. Deaf heard, the blind saw, the demoniacs were delivered, the traditionalists threw away their fetishes, idol-worshippers and the unregenerate backed out of darkness and received Jesus as Lord and Savior. Through him, Jesus and His power were manifested. And this continued all through the life span of his ministry. One thing was distinctive about him, as my mother, who was raised by him, attested; he was a man mighty in the place of prayer and fasting.

In my time and ministries as pastor and chaplain, many breakthroughs have been experienced by people in travail and problems who the Lord had directed my way. In the process of dealing with these issues, oftentimes, the Holy Spirit had ordered fasting-accompanied prayers, which ultimately brought deliverances, healings, supplies, and peace. I'm very sure that many faithful servants of God who heeded this powerful code have experienced God in such unusual ways that, according to the letters of Christ Himself, such can come forth by nothing but by prayer and fasting (Mark 9:29).

7. **Consecutiveness of prayer with fasting.** This topic differs a little bit from the persistence ingredient of prayer. In consecutiveness of praying with fasting, we want to look at a prayer with fasting that wants to be maximized by continuing for a certain length of time with no break. This is a scenario of a sporadic nonstop prayer and for a fairly longer time. For instance, for a very pressing cause at hand, a seven-day prayer fast may be called. It may be a three-day fast. For some powerful people, it may be a twenty-one-day prayer fast, with seclusion from people and food.

Sometimes, the prayer fast may have a beginning day and no end, especially if it is arranged as a daily fasting mode. There is liberty to arrange it the way one is led by the Spirit or the way an individual determines to do it. But the key is that it continues for an extended time with no predetermined end.

Examples include the forty-day fast by Jesus (Matthew 4:1–2). Paul spoke about some fasting that may be similar to this mode in the way he described his situations: "In weariness and painfulness, in watchings often, in hunger and thirst, in fastings often, in cold and nakedness" (2 Corinthians 11:27, KJV). Daniel's twenty-one-day fasting could be in this special class (Daniel chapter 10).

In Nigeria and some parts of Africa, where there are serious needs, people are used to these kinds of prayers. There are Prayer Mountains designated for such spiritual ventures, where people can recede for days away from home and family comfort to stay before God in fasting and prayers.

There was a time in my life when I was confronted with a very serious need in 2004. I decided to go into a continuous daily prayer fasting. From the onset, I decided not to stop until the Lord answered me. At the end of six months, the Lord gave me an instruction that brought the supply of the need. I give glory to God. It was a tasking but a unique experience. Apart from the need being supplied, my spiritual antennae became very sharp. It became a very special, refreshing time in the Lord with more virtues added into my life.

Allen postulated from his own experience that spending this kind of time exclusively with God brings the power of God into your life. He wrote: "Those who have power with God—who are bringing deliverance to the sick and suffering and winnings souls to Christ—are appending much time along with God before they spend time with others."[40] His expression emphasizes the aloneness with God. This kind of prayer arrangements are often not done with other people. For a church, maybe a three-day fasting and prayer could be the maximum. For instance, when I was growing up (and I think it still continues till today), our church (CAC) usually involved all who would register willingly for a three-day prayer fasting to end the Lenten season, culminating at Good Friday. But for practical purposes, if it is extending beyond three (3) days, I believe "alone" will be a better route to take.

Perhaps the 120 people who gathered in the Upper Room at Jerusalem may be an exception though we are not sure if fasting was incorporated into their fellowship that lasted ten days before the arrival of the Holy Ghost (Acts chapter 2).

1. **Vigil.** There is something potently unique about vigil. Vigil is the act of stretching your prayers into the night hours. Nighttime praying is one act that is very important in the life of man but which many feel helpless or uninterested in. But we must

ask why many are helpless or do not show interest in it. The answer is actually the potency underscoring the secret of the night hours.

A very deep and careful study of scriptures has revealed certain facts about night hours that a believer should be curious about.

Even though the nighttime is a legitimate part of the hours that make a full day, and even though it is the stretch that God had ordained for men to sleep in order to be restored and refreshed for the day that must follow the night hours, yet we gather that the night hours is a time that is equally fraught with disasters and dangers.

Nighttime is a time of darkness when people with physical eyes are not graced to be apt to execute activities with ease. So, we discovered that it takes an extra effort for anyone to carry out human activities at the night hours. In contrast, night hours are easy times for spirit beings to operate because there is less opposition from normal men who are more active during daytime. Since the things we do not see are the ones that control the ones we see (2 Corinthians 4:18), it is a fact that most of the activities of the day are fixed and controlled by activities during the night. That is why good believers have made it a duty to do vigil-night prayers to ensure that the day following goes well.

That the nighttime is a precarious time is explained in scripture. Night is put in parallel with the time when thieves can visit, and such visitations are to kill, steal, or destroy. It is exemplified like the day of the Lord when vengeance would visit the unbelieving and ungodly (2 Peter 3:10, Matthew 24:43).

Nighttime, dead at night, midnight, etc., are times of visitation of retribution. The angel of destruction struck the households of Egypt at midnight, taking out the firstborns of the land. Following was wailing all over the country (Exodus 12:29). Lot was made drunk at night so the daughters could have their way with him in their own special scheme to procreate and extend the family lineage after surviving the incineration of Sodom and Gomorrah (Genesis 19:30–38). The prosperous but foolish farmer in the story told by Jesus had his soul demanded of him that night (Luke 12:20).

The psalmist intimated to us and cautioned us about the pestilences that walk in darkness; in fact, many of them are noisome. They could be very devastating and deadly. Spiritual forces, fowlers, and "beings" that operate in the cover of the dark are usually behind these mischiefs. They go about unleashing terror (Psalm 91:3, 6). That is their time because they are evil and operating in the dark. All things considered, no wonder the word of God metaphorically refers to nighttime as a time when weeping and crying endure (Psalm 30:6). As a matter of fact, one of the few good things about the night can sometimes be tampered with. The Lord created the moon to rule the night by giving it light, but the evil powers have also mastered the schemes to hire the moon to strike some by night instead of providing illumination. To safeguard his children, the spirit of the Lord recommended a prayer of refuge: "The sun shall not smite thee by day, nor the moon by night" (Psalm 121:6, KJV). The evil machinery of this world will do all in its power to maximize its escapades in the dark hours of the night. Surely, nighttime could be a time to be fatally offended (Mark 14:27). Those assigned to arrest Jesus would carry it out at night for fear of supporters' reprisal in the daytime.

In lieu of the potency of the night hours, I believe God has decided in an eternal attempt to neutralize the gory and deadly activities of Satan and his evil cortege to line up some divine assignments and activities also for the night hours. In addition to His own instituted assignment, it appears that some in the Kingdom—"the watchmen" and the likes—have been assigned to pick up spiritual arms during these times to counter the deadly offensive of the evil lucifugous operators.

For instance, the Bible records several theophanies, visions, and revelations during night hours to his preferred and chosen ministers. At these instances, secrets are revealed, followed by assignments that, when carried out, God's people intended to be victims become protected and eventually victorious (Daniel 2:9, Acts 18:9, Exodus chapter 12).

The whole of Psalm 91 is a credence to how those who trust in the Lord and stay with Him closely are referred to as those who dwell in the secret places of the Most High. Equally, they are the very ones who shall be preserved under the shadow of the Almighty. They are delivered from the fowlers and noisome pestilences, most of which walk in darkness and unleash terrors in the night hours. Many who are careless or who have not made the Lord their refuge become victims, and they could be numerous. Mercy is not in the arsenal of Satan and his lieutenants. But we are emboldened that if we key in to the protective plan of our Father God, with our eyes, we will see those ungodly and the wicked rewarded for their evil deeds and perpetrations.

During these dead hours, God has actually sent forces to rescue people who belong to Him. In Exodus chapter 12, in the hour that the Egyptian households were being torched with sudden death, God's people were not only selectively saved but were actually released from bondage with resources and money given to them in large supply by their slave masters and neighbors. God preserved, saved, rescued, released, and blessed them all in the same night when the Egyptians were being pummeled and pounded.

Much as the divine efficiency of angelic warfare would be a strong neutralizing factor in the night debacles between the opposing giant forces, God expects us humans to sometimes rise up and take part in these night battles as He vows to give us strength. He is the strength of our lives so we cannot be intimidated or afraid (Psalm 27:1–3).

Take a look at Jesus; after He had performed some miracles on the Sabbath day, the Scribes and Pharisees became indignant and actually began to plot against Him. Knowing what they were up to, He receded to a private place on the mountain and continued all night in praying unto God. In our modern-day term, He had an all-night prayer vigil. Following the all-night prayer, greater powers came upon Him. Let's observe the events that followed: In divine wisdom, He selected and called some apostles to disciple, came to the plain with them surrounded by a large crowd from diverse territories—Judea, Jerusalem, Tyre, and Sidon. They gladly heard the gospel. Many were saved while others were healed of their diseases; those with demon possessions were freed of those unclean and demonic spirits while many were touching Him to be imparted with virtue, which clearly was being released of Him. In short, the night vigil brought a windfall of miracles, signs, and wonders!

We know that God would always give His beloved sleep at night for the majority because it is the ordained time of rest and refreshing so His children could be very functional during the day (Psalm 127:2). However, we also know that because of the dangers inherent in the fallout of the night warfare, God would station some of the Kingdom anointed watchmen to keep watch during the night hours (Ezekiel 33:6-7, Isaiah 62:6-7). Thus, David intimated to us of such a profitable vocation: "Bless ye the LORD, all ye servants of the LORD, which by night stand in the house of the LORD. Lift up your hands in the sanctuary, and bless the LORD" (Psalm 134:1–2, KJV). Then, the Lord that made the heaven and earth, the Great Man of war, the Lord of Hosts, the Holy One of Israel will bless us out of Zion (Psalm 134:3). Some of these blessings include routing our enemies before us and granting us peace and prolonged life of accomplishing our purpose (Psalm 91:16).

These are men of God who would watch and often receive words and knowledge and prophecies from the Lord and transfer them to God's children from time to time to warn, forestall, and empower against the enemies of the soul.

In every generation, God has given us examples of men who are powerful in the night hours.

And when the inhabitants of Jabeshgilead heard of that which the Philistines had done to Saul;

All the valiant men arose, and went all night, and took the body of Saul and the bodies of his sons from the wall of Bethshan, and came to Jabesh, and burnt them there.

And they took their bones, and buried them under a tree at Jabesh, and fasted seven days.
1 Samuel 31:11–13 (KJV)

These valiant (powerful, bold, armed, and courageous) men defied the oddity of the night to do honor to the anointed men for the sake of God. They understood that God's honor, wherever demanded, must be upheld and preserved. Night vigil prayer warriors in the sight of God are valiant men who fight the night marauders arrayed against God, His children, and His purposes.

Nehemiah and a few chosen men, plus his donkey, acted in like manner and rode all night to view the current state of an assignment that God had given them (Nehemiah 2:12–16). The only time they could do it well to avoid the enemy interference was at night. Such a venture, just like night vigil, requires men and women who are in tune with the understanding of what job needs to be done, what battles need to be fought, what rescue operations need to be carried out, and at what hours of the day or night, no matter how odd. And indeed, without excuses, those assignments must be carried out. The dubious tag on the night as a time not to joke with or desire is finally highlighted with its exclusion from our final destination—the New Jerusalem: Paradise, the ultimate destination and home of all God's children redeemed from all the earth. We are encouraged: "And the city [the New Jerusalem] had no need of the sun, neither of the moon, to shine in it: for the glory of God did lighten it, and the Lamb is the light thereof. And there shall be no night there…" (Revelation 21:23, 22:5a). But in the time being, prayers offered through the night hours are very powerful and offensive laden against evil forces that set array against God's people. That is why some of the Gospel and Pentecostal churches of today have it in their preferred services. As a matter of effective operation, a night vigil prayer must encompass the hours that cross into past midnight.

It is around the time when night crawlers, either in the flesh or spirit, set out to begin their night marauding. It is the time when forces clash with forces. But ironically, it is the time the sleep can also weigh down on people who are apt to be victims of negative spiritual forces.

I encourage every Christian family to at least engage in occasional midnight prayers, maybe weekly or monthly, in the home setting or in the church setting. No believer should indulge himself a pass on this. If Christ did it while on earth, I'm convinced it is very essential for you and me. Paul and Silas did it in jail while awaiting the axe men. God released an angel from heaven and freed them

(Acts chapter 16). Peter was almost a toast to Herod. The church came together in some very serious prayers that extended to the wee hours of the morning. Angels were dispatched to release Peter. He actually came out to meet them at the night vigil. Prayer on that special night changed gear into praise vigil, with more blessings pouring like a shower upon the vigilers and the entire church. Imagine the extended benefits and blessings of getting the lives of Peter, Paul, and Silas saved!

2. **Prayer lining up with the will of God.** No prayer is more favored than one said to ask for what God has planned and decided to do. Such prayer is simply an activator and a boost. It is a blessing 101. It is a prayer that is most powerful because the power of prayer is not in the muscle with which it is voiced or articulated but rather in the result it produces and the manner the result is pleasing to the Lord.

Apostle John gave us this clear-cut device. He declared that there is a matter of unmatched confidence that when we ask anything according to God's will, He hears us, and if God can hear us say in prayer something He had scripted to do, such is a done deal.

Man, I pray I'm taught of the spirit of God those things that God has earmarked for me so I can pray them with such a spiritual accuracy and experience God's outpouring of the manifestation. In the book

90 Minutes in Heaven, Don Piper reported of how the spirit of the Lord told Dick Onerecker to pray for his dead, mangled body inside his crashed car by Livingston River Bridge.[41] It was an interesting account. Dick was a Baptist minister who admitted that what the Lord was telling him to do was contra to his theological belief. He did not believe that one could pray for a dead body to be received back to life. But I believe apart from the fact that God had determined to raise up Don Piper from the dead and needed someone to be used, He also wanted to demonstrate His power for Dick to experience an opportunity to believe God for bigger works. In spite of his shallow theology on the matter, the urge was very compelling, and he moved to say the prayers upon his friend Don, and to his bewilderment, he started to move, and Don is the author of the story. It was intriguing. Faith, fasting, vigil, and all other ingredients were not in play here, but God already had a finished agenda that Dick was called to execute. Result: A person who never believed that power gifts are for today became the "miracle worker." Therefore, prayer said to activate the will of God is powerful and availing.

3. **Praying the word of God.** Praying the word of God releases an unbeatable power into our prayers. The scripture tells us: "Forever, O Lord, your word is settled in heaven" (Psalm 119:89, NKJV). This implies that every written (Logos) and spoken (*Rhema*) word from God is confirmed permanent in the Heavenlies, and if so, on earth,

it is done. Nothing can reverse it. Concerning the pronouncements of God, the word testifies of itself that "heaven and earth may pass away, but My Word will not" (paraphrased) (Matthew 24:35, NKJV).

The word of God possesses the power to create. It brings to life and existence things that are far beyond man's creative genius, power, and ideas. The word of God brought the creations to life in the first five days that God worked for creation purposes—the day, sun, moon, stars, night, seas, land, trees, animals, birds, resources under the ground, etc. All that man would need on earth for existence were brought forth through the Lord's voicing out, "Let there be..." and things named began to come into existence (Genesis 1:3–25). Apostle Peter later signed off on this fact when he reminded us that all we need for life and godliness has been provided through the knowledge of Jesus Christ, who called us to glory and virtue (2 Peter 1:3). And Christ is the word (John 1:1–5), by whom all things were created.

In the prophecy of Isaiah the prophet, the unstoppable power of functionality of the word of God was likened to the rain waters that pour down over the earth from the sky. It cannot return, but it proceeds to soak and drench the land and causes it to bring forth plants, trees, and crops of all sorts, which, at the time of harvest, will supply food for men to eat and seeds for planting in the next season. The words of God that have been spoken will surely do what they were spoken to do. That is exactly the secret behind the success of a man who has mastered the art of praying God's words (cf. Isaiah 55:9–11).

Let's look at a few examples of words concerning very important areas of our lives that can be repeated in prayer for uttermost efficiency:

Peace—John 14:1—Lord, I can't be troubled because I believe in You, and I believe in God. My heart will not be troubled, in Jesus' name.

John 14:27—Dear Lord, I belong to You. I receive the peace that You have offered me. It is not like the peace the world gives, but Your peace that is lasting, I receive in Jesus' name.

Healing—Isaiah 53:4–5—Dear Lord Jesus, You have surely borne my grief and carried my sorrow… You have been wounded for my transgressions; You were bruised for my iniquities: the chastisement of my peace was upon You, and with Your stripes, I am healed in Jesus' name.

Provision—Philippians 4:19—Dear Father, You are my God; You shall supply all my needs according to Your riches in glory by Christ Jesus, in Jesus' name.
Wealth—Deuteronomy 8:18—Dear Lord, You are my God. I acknowledge You as the Giver of power to make wealth. Lord, grant me the power to make

wealth so You can establish Your covenant with me, in Jesus' name.

Psalm 1—Dear Lord, because I belong to You, You will prosper everything I touch in Jesus' name.

Possessing eternal life—John 3:16, 1 John 5:11–12—Dear Lord, I believe in Your beloved Son, Jesus Christ. Therefore, I receive eternal life in Jesus' name.

Faced with threats and dangers—Psalm 118:17—Dear Father God, I shall not die but live and declare the works of the Lord in the land of the living, in Jesus' name.

Security against enemies and attacks—Isaiah 54:17—My Father, in the name of Jesus, I declare that no weapons fashioned against me shall be effective, and I stand to condemn every tongue raised up against me, amen.

Help—Isaiah 50:5, Psalm 46:1—My Father and my God, I look to You; You are my very present help. Lord, You will help me in Jesus' name.

My family's success and living a strong and victorious life—Isaiah 8:18—Dear Lord, me and my children are for signs and wonders from You, the Lord of Hosts, in this land, in Jesus' name.

Success in academics—1 John 2:20, 27—My Father in heaven, I have an unction from Your spirit. I profess that I master excellently all my works and reading in Jesus' name. Dear Holy Spirit, You have been assigned to be my Helper and Teacher; help and teach me. I receive all the knowledge You are imparting into me for a great success in my academics in Jesus' name.

As God's enlightened children, it is expedient for us to take advantage of this powerful ingredient of prayer. The Words Ministries' idea put into writing on this subject matter is very complimentary: Prayer is not a religious form without power. It is accurate, effective, and result oriented. Prayer is the "living" word in your mouth. Because God watches over His words, if you stuff your mouth with God's words, your prayer is very powerful. It is therefore vindicating that another portion in the collection of the sayings of God attests that the prayer of the believer (righteous) is efficacious (James 5:16).

Find God's pronouncements that relate to your issues and begin to pray them just as the few I have given you. You will begin to enjoy special grace of your Father God in the place of supplication. I assure you that by committing to praying God's words that you stand no chance of praying amiss, of harboring fear of noncorrelation with God's plan for your life, of offering powerless and noneffective prayers, and of not receiving answers to your prayers.

Go for it; pray applicable God's word.

CHAPTER 8:

WHEN GOD ANSWERS BY NOT ANSWERING

The blessings later acquired from "unanswered prayer" is a proof after the fact that no prayer escapes the considering ears and the mind of God. Makes me remember a hymn by Mary Bernstecher: "He will answer every prayer, / God has given you His promise, / That He hears and answers prayer, / He will heed your supplication, / If you cast on Him your care. / Go to Him in faith believing, / He will answer every prayer."

The finite man entreating the infinite God in prayer must assume total faith, without question, in the fairness and love of God as a Father. God is too knowing, too faithful, too caring, too loving, and infinitely committed to His image-like creation to not hear and answer when they call on Him in prayers.

Philip Yancey told a story of Karl, a retired air force officer and former chaplain who, because of a sudden accident in his neighborhood not in the war zone, became three-quarters paralyzed. It was a very moving story. I referenced the story because of its perfect fit with the topic we are expounding on in this chapter.

According to Yancey, Karl, a neighbor, was a retired Air Force lieutenant colonel serving as a chaplain in a long-term care home. He used to work out regularly in an attempt to keep up with the young, physically fit recruits. Now he rolls his wheelchair down the hallways visiting senior citizens, some bedbound, some broken by dementia. Every thirty minutes, an alarm goes off, and he lifts himself up by arm strength alone and then sets his motionless lower half down in a different position to prevent pressure sores. Yancey recalled: "I visited Karl at work and later at home, and both times, our conversation reverted to the topic of God's silence, something that is a way of saying 'God's answering by not answering' or 'by not saying anything.'" The story continued.

Karl had a bicycle accident in which he landed on his helmet, crushing vertebrae and damaging the spiral cord. Since then, he had been paralyzed from the chest down, causing his air force career to end. From then on, physical therapy replaced his normal workout routine. He voiced out how difficult it was for him to begin to come to terms with his new status: a "disabled" man. He relayed to Yancey a lot of adjustments that he had to make, but there was one that was particularly and extremely difficult. In addition to the numerous whys he threw at God, it was the withdrawal of God's presence that was a blockbuster. He couldn't get it. Just when he really needed God most, God disappeared.

It was hard enough to guess answers to questions like why God would allow him, who was serving others faithfully in His name, showing and imparting the love and care of God, to have such a career and almost life-ending accident even in the neighborhood. If it was in the midair, maybe it would have been better understood. Why would God not prevent all these and then, on top of the dilemma, decide to just bail? In his words, "Just when I need God most, I can no longer sense Him. I keep on praying and believing, but it is as if I'm praying to the ceiling. I get no response."[42] This period lasted about one year of mental torture, but eventually, God, he believes, began to show glimpses of not totally abandoning him. He took a trip to Taizé Community in France. With the switches of a week in silence, a week in community prayer service, centering on meditations and prayer, he began to experience such a gripping spiritual experience, the type he had never ever experienced in his life. He began to swim in God's presence, with which this community has been permeated. He remarked, "Perhaps God gave me that experience to anchor me for what was to follow."

Invariably after his return, Karl now came to be led into some of the psalms of David that speak of very challenging times in his life. He seemed to connect with these psalms of prayer that permitted him to speak his own lament:

How long o Lord will you forget me? Forever?

How long will you hide your face from me?

How long must I wrestle with my thoughts and everyday have sorrow in my heart?

But if I go to the east, he is not there;

If I go to the west, I do not find him.

When he is at work n the north, I do not see him;

When he turns to the south, I catch no glimpse of him.

O my God, I cry out by day but you do not answer,

By night, and am not silent.

… ……my soul taunt me,

Saying to me all day long,

"Where is your God?"

I spread out my hands to you;

My soul thirst for you like a parched land.

Yancy confessed that after this visitation with Kaul, he, too, began to pay attention to some of these biblical writings and psalms that a casual reader has a tendency to take just as fictional prayers. But these are plaintive prayers that come as cries from the soul of real men who actually passed through fire in their life sojourn, addressed to the God who, at that time, seems deaf or wholly absent. This account? Moving but educative.

Advanced studying of scripture, however, has revealed to us that those ten to twelve years in between the anointing of David by Samuel and the time he was coronated in Hebron and finally at Jerusalem were seasons of travail. Some of those times, God could virtually not be found, and sometimes, He would show up to let David know that the plans have not been scrapped. I believe every one of us must, at some point in our lives, grasp with a story of a man like David, a man after God's own heart, seeing the crescendo of his life as he went through the valleys and wilderness and sketches in time when it appeared like God was out of scene, but eventually, the end was worth the promise, and the fulfillment of God's providence was confirmed.

Such an episode provides words for us today. In the course of our walk with God in this life, for as long as we will have the need to pray, more than likely, we will experience times and seasons when God will appear not to be answering our supplication, though, in reality, it does not mean that He is not. It's the strong perception because of the circumstances surrounding the stretch of life.

Regardless of how a man feels in situations where God is doing His own thing, God is hardly fazed. Because He is a good God and because man would see ultimately His goodness, though, at the point, they may not know from where God is coming, He sticks to His agenda and workings.

The key point that must be a lesson learned in this chapter is that we must stand with God trusting, knowing that He is there though the air may be silent. While the silence persists, we must be persuaded that God is working in our situation. One thing I've discovered from a careful study of peoples' situation that went through a lull of this sort is that God had come through with a bigger timed result. Let's look at a few case points:

Abraham obtained a promise at age seventy-five. For twenty-five years, he and his wife, Sarah, went through a period of unending expectations. The longer the wait, the more insensible the reality of what was promised. A couple of those ages cannot be hopeful of reproducing as the time rolls. The older they get, the lesser the probability of the capability to reproduce. In their desperation, they almost settled for Ishmael as the promised child, but God's own promise and plan would not bulge. In the end, God broke the "silence." Sarah conceived at age ninety and had Isaac, the real child of promise. Ultimately, the child was worth the wait. He fits the spiritual character of one that would bring to light the promise given to his father, Abraham (Genesis chapters 21 to 28).

Hannah went to Shiloh every year to worship God and sought God's face in prayer for a child. A good and godly woman loved by her husband, Elkanah, who would do anything for this loving woman except that her greatest desire is a need that no man can supply but God. Many years of waiting was agonizing, especially as the other woman mocked her for her childlessness and her trust in the God of Israel, which appeared to be futile. God did not seem to care about the plight of His loving and faithful daughter. But unknowing to us all, God had in His hand a tri-star for her: a child who would lead God's nation, be the prime mouthpiece of God, and install kings. Most definitely, the child would equate many.

Hannah stuck with God trusting and supplicating while keeping her comportment even in the face of a brush with Eli the priest who, instead of the pronouncer of her blessing he eventually became, would have been a detractor. Praise the Lord, Samuel the child was born: a prophet, judge, and kings' maker, a mighty man through whom the godly woman and mother of faith, Hannah, was forever defined. God came through with a higher price for her wait and years of silence.

Lazarus, the friend of Jesus, fell badly sick. He already had the break anyone yearned for; for he had as a friend a miracle worker, the son of God for whom nothing is impossible. At the snap of the finger, the sisters would get Jesus to come and heal Lazarus. But far from the human logical thinking, God has a different plan, though the end would be the same or even more gratifying. But you know, in our walk of faith, we are more focused on the immediate.

Even when we are more than sure that the end is beautiful, we still trip up on the present afflictions that seem to get the better part of us today. I'm reminded of

Paul's encouragement in his epistle to the Corinthians: "For our light affliction, which is but for a moment, worketh for us a far more exceeding and eternal weight of glory" (2 Corinthians 4:17, KJV). It is ironic but conclusively gratifying how the present pain, hardship, and unexplainable deals we receive from God now are building for us a bigger, more satisfying delivery later. Only God has the answer. Paul proceeded further to encourage us using the imagery of how the things we see or feel now are very temporary, that is, they won't last forever, but God already reserved (though we can't see or feel it now) for us a bigger result that cannot fail (verse 18).

Continuing with the story, the friend Lazarus had in Jesus would not show up because He had more pressing job to do. It would be perfectly in order for the sisters Mary and Martha to query in their hearts what more urgent assignment would be there for the deliverer save a man and a friend on his way out. Many a time, in our low moments, we ask in our hearts what God was up to. "What better issue was on HHis mind than me being redeemed by the blood of Jesus, who is supposed to be the apple of His eyes? How could He refuse to show up in my situation or talk to me or rescue me or provide for me?"

The delay went on and resulted in the undesirable visitation by the last enemy of man, death. The atmosphere burned sour for the family that had often entertained and fed Jesus. How could Jesus have done that? But thank God for time, for it is a wound healer. We would later understand the mind of Christ, that knowing all things, He was confident that Lazarus was only sleeping (in reality) because when the Resurrection and the Life is in the vicinity, those who belong to God cannot die (John 11:25). Secondly, Jesus knew that the worse it got, the greater the glory it would bring to God (verse 4).

Eventually, Jesus came after four days when Lazarus was already buried, and the body had started to smell. He proceeded to call him out of the grave, and his life was restored. The divine intervention here was monumentally big. It became a miracle of its kind; not many who had been long dead were recorded raised. In the end, many were saved—"Then many of the Jews which came to Mary [to mourn for the dead], and had seen the things that Jesus did, believed on him" (John 11:45, KJV). Even many carried the news beyond, announcing what wonders the Lord had performed, which later would entice many to come back and see Jesus, with the prospect of getting saved or healed or blessed. Again, God did not react the way we would have loved Him to, for why would He act in a way to cause pain and anguish and sorrow for those four days when the family experienced the real and practical pains of losing a loved one in Lazarus? But ultimately, the blessings, the joy, the saved lives, and the magnitude of the miracle all was indeed worth the wait and the experience.

Jesus Himself, the beloved Son of God, tasted His own medicine from the hand of His Father God. At the Garden of Gethsemane, looking at the brutality ahead for Him in three days, He appealed for a possible change of plans. No-yes answer was forthcoming. At the cross, while the travail peaked, Jesus expressed loneliness and desertion: "My God, my God, why have you forsaken me?" (Mark 15:33, NIV) Later we were told why—for God had a bigger payday out of the unparalleled drama. Billions of souls were on the line to be saved and reconciled to God if Christ would pull it through. Thank God He did and became the author of salvation bringing mankind back to God, their Maker.

The Father was so pleased with Him that He gave Him a name that is above every other name on earth and in heaven and that at His name, every knee should bow and every tongue confess that He is Lord. What a beautiful destination to a difficult road traveled!

Don Piper, the Houston preacher who died in a car crash on a Northeast Harris County bridge and was later raised, in his book *90 Minutes in Heaven*, recalled how at a point during his long recovery became so frustrated, discouraged, and depressed.[43] Imagine a person lying on one side for thirteen months not able to move. That was simply unreal. In this tired state, he prayed that the Lord would take his life. He was simply down and out. To him, there was no ray of hope. He was convinced he could not make it. He queried why God would bring him back alive and passionately prayed that God would pull the plug.

But God was virtually silent and did not answer.

However, later we knew that the "no answer" was a good answer. Today, his life had become a testimony, and many have been lifted up by what God did for him. The pains, the sadness, and the depression have been lived through, and the power of God could be attested to, and like David, he could say severally: "Come and see what the Lord has done for me" (Psalm 34:8).

My first attempt at obtaining a visa to come to the United States was not successful. I did not feel good about that. I was very angry with God. I believed He let me down. There was no reason why I would not obtain the visa. I prayed and trusted God. But He failed me. I decided, in my frustration and pain, that I wouldn't pray to God anymore. At the passage of time, I snailed my way back to my usual way of relating to God, and we became cool again.

It wasn't until two years later when the Lord beautifully gave me the visa and brought me into the country, that I began to realize that the timing of my crossing over was surely fixed by God. I began to understand that had I come two years earlier, my life might have taken a very different direction as opposed to the way it worked out when I later came. As God had ordained and directed my path, I had experienced the call of God upon my life, with the Lord giving me a ministry, and had committed many into my care to minister to and cater for. Obviously, the two years had been a tiebreaker; no one could convince me otherwise. Though it was tough and challenging, it felt like I was in disarray; now, I know that the two waiting years worked for a better future for me that began to unfold thereafter.

I'm convinced that my time, in the words of David, is in the hands of God (Psalm 31:15). Most assuredly, I can say that He is a master at managing a life to success in accordance with His original plans. I can go on citing many examples revealing the goodness and the caring of God in situations that tempt us to believe that God does not care at times, that His eyes and ears are selectively closed and blocked against us whenever He feels like. Understanding what God is doing in our situations is very important.

Whenever we enter into our wilderness, which all of us will at one time or another in the course of living on earth, it is important to seek to understand what the Lord is up to and how He is feeling towards our situation. This is very important for us because it helps us to settle the question of what to do with prayer as a tool with which we will deal with our situation. When the Lord seems quiet after you have been pounding the throne of grace with prayer, you've got to get to the point where you know that your prayers are being answered with silence, or you need to continue to pray perseveringly until the Lord will bring an answer.

Some of the factors that can be helpful to take us to the point of settling the issue include:

1. Having faith in the Lord that regardless of the outcome, I belong to Him and that He is my father.

2. Examining yourself to be sure that you are in good

standing with God. Paul admonishes us to examine ourselves to see whether we are in the faith (Corinthians 13:5). In the season when we feel like God is not answering, it is confidence-inducing to confirm our standing right with God.

3. We must seek to have the knowledge of what is. No better information could surpass that which the Holy Spirit gives to us. He is the One who knows the mind of God. Divine revelation will show us what we need to know or have or do. In addition, contemporary, scientific, and general knowledge can be very discerning. We are told: "My people perish for lack of knowledge."

4. Understanding the situation we are in and the information and knowledge that have been supplied can be invaluable in deciphering what is on the ground. Understanding of facts may suggest what needs to be done or undone to complement divine intervention when it has been released.

Paul encourages us in the eighth chapter of his epistle to the Romans very greatly. All things he confirms work out for good of them that love the Lord and are called according to His purpose (verse 28). So, when I hit a stretch that is turbulent, I stop and examine myself: Do I love the Lord? Am I showing caring attitude towards things of God? Is my life operating in consonance with the principles of God? If all these are yes, then I have the peace that the Lord is surely with me. Though I may not hear any sound, nevertheless, I am convinced that by His grace, my tears will survive the night, and morning will appear to supply me with a divine break. I know that my God will not tarry forever.

Knowing that His plans for me are good and not bad, to bless and not impoverish, to give me hope and an expected end, I know I will pull it through by His grace (Jeremiah 29:11). I'm persuaded that the Lord, who began this great work in me, will surely complete it, for He is able and reputable to beautifully complete every good work that He committedly started in me.

Our God is good always to all who belong to Him and who place their trust and confidence in Him.

CHAPTER 9:
INTERCESSION

What you make happen to others, God will make happen for you. Pray for someone today, for in this act of thinking about and caring for another, the providence of God will locate you.

Intercession is the prayer offered by someone else for us or on our behalf. It is also the one we pray for another person. This we may or may not know, but the focal point is that the prayer is from another person.

God, in His infinite operations and management of the humans, created a space for intercessions. We are proudly informed that it is an act that is pleasing to Him (1 Timothy 2:1–8). In other words, God is happy when a person prays for another, with or without their knowledge. The most appropriate situation of intercession is when the one being lifted up in prayer is not in the vicinity of the intercessor. The intercessor is the one doing the prayer.

Intercession was invented by God because He knew that

as we pass through life, there will be times, stretches, and situations in our lives when the prayer of others is the anchor that will stabilize us or pull us through. Bear in mind that there are certain portions of the divine provisions, releases, supply, care, and manifestations that will not be experienced except prayers are offered. This fact is reiterated by Christ, the Son of God Himself, when He prayed on numerous occasions. He taught us prayers and mandated us to pray, albeit incessantly. But the question rears up as to how a man will subsist when he is not in a position or capacitated to pray for himself or pray adequately. I believe it is in these kinds of situations that the Lord invented and created a room for recognizing that some others must pray for one and vice versa. Intercession is needful in the church and in the community of God's people.

That God loves intercession is confirmed by the fact that when intercessors are not engaged in prayer, God is grieved. In the time of Prophet Isaiah's ministration in Israel (see chapter 59), the spirit of the Lord revealed the wretchedness and abhorrence of the lives of God's people, of how they are down in the abyss of transgression and sin and were being buried alive by the windfall of their state of separation from God (verse 2). God expressed of how their hands are stained with blood and their fingers with guilt, of their lying lips and tongues muttering wickedness. They had no integrity. They took pride in fomenting troubles and birthing evil. He figuratively described their sordidness, liking their continuous lifestyles as hatching the eggs of vipers and spinning spider's web. Sadly, the Lord continued ironically, whoever ate the eggs died (obviously of the deadly serpentine poison), and when the eggs hatched naturally, vipers and serpents were brought forth, creating a very dangerous and unsafe landscape of habitation! What kind of cover would a spider's web provide for man? Yet, in their folly of ungodliness, that is what they spin. No wonder they will be naked in the cold. Because their feet rush into sin and their thoughts are continually evil, they cannot identify the way of sin, let alone avoid walking in them. Many more of these treacheries did the Lord exclaimed (in Isaiah chapter 59), but the peak of God's outlash was found in verses 15b to 16a (NIV): "The Lord looked and was displeased that there was no justice. He saw that there was no one to intervene [intercede, KJV]."

Obviously, with all that was going on in the land, and if that was not heartbreaking enough, the fact that all slept with their heads in the same direction and not even a single person could muster the spirit into the realm of interceding for the multitude of sinners was like the last nail in their coffins. Sealed! And God couldn't take it anymore! But in a sweet twist and proving my point, God Himself decided to act as the intercessor:

> *[...] so his own arm achieved salvation for him, and his own righteousness sustained him. He put on righteousness as his breastplate and the helmet of salvation on his head; he put on the garments of vengeance*

and wrapped himself in zeal as in a cloak.
[The Redeemer will come to Zion, to those in
Jacob who repent of their sins.]

Isaiah 16b–17 (NIV)

Intercession is in the "blood" of God (Isaiah 53:12). He loves to rescue and lend a helping hand. He is our refuge and strength, a very present help in trouble (Psalm 46:1).

If God loves intercession, He demands it from us; most definitely, He is delighted in the intercessors. Apostle Paul exhorts the brethren in Thessalonica: "Pray for us that the message of the Lord may spread rapidly and be honored, just as it was with you" (2 Thessalonians 3:1, NIV). And pray that we may be delivered from wicked and evil men (2 Thessalonians 3:1–2). In Hebrew 13:18, he humbly requested intercession that he may be released from prison and join God's people where he would continue to freely do the work of the gospel. Banking on their prayers and believing that the Lord would answer, he even requested Philemon to prepare a room where he would lodge after his release (verse 22).

Apostle James encouraged believers to pray one for another that those who are sick may be healed (James 5:16). There may be self-prayers where strength and energy still are. But it would appear that God gives an allocation of effectiveness for intercession in the formula of divine intervention. Of course, given are those situations where self capacity in prayer to deal with issue at hand is very low and inadequate or even nonexistent, wherein intercession would appear to be the only way out.

That was the case when Peter was arrested and projected to be executed following Herod's success at taking out James. The church convened into some uninterrupted extended intercessions for their leader Peter. For a man on a death row, not much can be expressed concerning his own personal zeal to pray. But in response to the pounding of the throne of mercy by the brethren in the place of prayer, God dispatched a monumental rescue mission that freed Peter (Acts chapter 12).

While the Israelites were on their way to the Promised Land, on numerous occasions, Moses had to intercede for his subjects at moments when God's anger would bring fierce retribution upon them. They had been spared numerously when these occurred (Exodus 15:22–27, Numbers chapter 14).

The power of intercession lies in the arena that God will heed the prayer of one at a particular time either because he is favored or in the right disposition to be heard of the Lord, as opposed to the one that needs the prayer or because one is in the exclusive position to intercede so the one needing the prayer may be rescued or restored. The latter was the case with Moses and the children of Israel or, generally, when the more righteous had to pray for the less.

Another glaring example was when Elymas the Sorcerer implored Paul to intercede for him so that the impending curse upon him would be reverted (Act 8:24). In a perverted state of mind he was operating, he had requested to pay for the gifts of the Holy Spirit so he could continue in his evil practice. In response, Paul cursed him. It then would seem that only Paul was in the position to intercede for him.

Peter and the interceding church would fit the earlier profile. Peter could pray for himself, and he might have prayed, though to what extent we do not know. He was not in any controversial situation that one could suggest that God may not want to listen to him. But in spite, the room for the prayers of other saints to work for him was a special allocation that partly sums up the inherent power of intercession, as earlier mentioned. That is why no matter how strong we are spiritually, the prayers of others for us have a special room in our life to fill.

Will Malgo, as a matter of fact, boosted the outlook of intercession at its best, calling it a life-giving prayer for another and endeavoring to share what he sees as the secret of its potency. To be an effective intercessor, he challenges a would be to identify with the one you are praying for: "Make yourself one in spirit with the spiritually dead person. Throw yourself down before God and cry to him without ceasing. Persevere and let your willingness to die for others be wholehearted." The missive calls for doubling down when he observes that "many give up so soon."[44]

The prayer of others for us will continue to enjoy success from God, and that is why we all must aspire to be intercessors for another, no matter of what degree. Apart from being a direct blessing, God's favor upon intercessors is vivid for some reasons:

1. **Intercessors are partners with God on Kingdom success.** God has His great agendas that He executes through the church. Those that He uses are often challenged by the devil and his cohorts. That is why major officers of the Kingdom must be kept in perpetual prayers (intercession). Paul demands that believers in all churches pray (intercede) not only for one another but steadfastly for kings, leaders, and all those in authority in churches, homes, and everywhere God's business is connected, that all may live peaceful, quiet lives in all godliness and holiness. "This is good, and pleases God our Savior [he continued], who wants all people to be saved and to come to a knowledge of the truth. And for this purpose I was appointed a herald and an apostle..." (1 Timothy 2:3–5, 7a, NIV). Look at the causes and the benefits mentioned here that intercession would command to life: peace, godliness, salvation, efficacy of the apostles and the preachers of the gospel, etc. These are high-profile issues of the Kingdom. The Lord has to favor those who, through prayers, make them happen.

2. **Building the body of Christ.** Deriving from all those causes brings multiplier effects to the church. More of the godly members and efficient gifted leaders lead to effective, strong, and vibrant body of Christ.

3. **Intercessor's interceding is an indirect way of helping oneself.** There is the age-long life principle of *"whatever you make happen for others, God will make happen for you."* Delving into pure spiritual line, praying for another, generates a divinely executed intercession for you. Remember Paul: "Be not deceived; God is not mocked: for whatsoever a man soweth, that shall he also reap" (Galatians 6:7, KJV). Sow intercession into a life that is needy; reap encouragement and a divine intervention at your moments of need. "Blessed is he that considereth the poor [the psalmist writes]: the LORD will deliver him in time of trouble. The LORD will preserve him, and keep him alive; and he shall be blessed upon the earth: and thou wilt not deliver him unto the will of his enemies. The LORD will strengthen him upon the bed of languishing: thou wilt make all his bed in his sickness" (Psalm 41:1–3, KJV). Job prayed for his friends, who had misanalyzed his situation, coming under God's indignation. After his intercession, God restored and twice blessed him (Job chapter 42). Jesus, in John chapter 17, prayed a lot for His disciples that they may be one. They eventually succeeded Him and continued to preach Him starting in Jerusalem, to Judea, to Samaria, and to the uttermost end of the earth.

4. **Intercession minimizes the tentacles of Satan.** Praying for others to clip the wings of the archenemy in situations where he would otherwise have had easy preys and banked another victory.

Intercession for another child of God under attack is what reinforcement is to an infantry at war. Reinforcements give a battalion extra firepower and so a stronger hand upon the enemy. As a result, victory comes much handy, thus increasing the life span of soldiers in peril. Therefore, in a comparable manner, intercession brings divine deliverance to incarcerated saints. As intercession expands, lives are saved from eternal death, rescued from Satan's claw, stabilized in faith, and freedom from sin becomes accessible. In addition, prayer warriors get stronger, and forces of hell get weaker because greater is He who is in us than he that is without (1 John 4:4).

Jesus Christ in Matthew 5:44 (KJV) enjoins us: "Love your enemies, bless them that curse you, do good to them that hate you, and pray for them which despitefully use you, and persecute you…" To please the Lord in this regard, one has got to be gusty, but the benefit is obvious. The patience that enables a man to pray for the ungodly could become the element that increases the chance of him coming to Christ in salvation. This is a direct derivative: when it occurs, the kingdom of hell loses membership while heaven records a gain. Such is the power of intercession.

Chuck Holton wrote a memoir titled *The Photo That Answered a Prayer* that is a fit here. The retired military man started by dropping this rhetoric: "When is a picture worth more than a thousand words?" The answer is a direct experience of the parents of a Marine sergeant involved in the Iraq war. For them, a combat photo and a battlefront letter proved that God had heard their prayers. Most definitely, their intercession for their son did not go unattended to by God. One of the most powerful and widely seen images of that war—the image of Marine Sergeant Jesse Lanter carrying an injured fellow marine off the battlefield—was the direct answer to the prayers continuously offered by worried parents of Lanter, who desperately yearned to be assured that their son was okay in the volatile war front thousands of miles away from home.[45]

David and Alyson knew Jesse was somewhere, probably at the war front alive (the best imagination). They needed some kind of way to know for sure that was so. They prayed: "God, please just point him out, one time." Soon after, newspapers across the country carried the famous photograph of their son, Jesse, rescuing Corporal Barry Lange at a standoff in Al Bayer, near Basra. And the father said, "And in the print under the picture, to be able to read where he was, and see in print, and to be able to follow him from there on out, it was to me an answer to prayer."

To many who saw those picture, it was just a general storyline, but to David and Alyson Lanter, parents of Jesse, God honors intercession. Those prayers offered for their son, as answered by God, were a lifesaver from worry, apprehension, and lack of genuine peace. "We just want to give God the glory for saving Jesse's soul."

With that part of prayer answered, their faith has been reinforced to continue to pray for his safe final arrival, with many young sons of other parents, even some who may not be disposed to praying. That oblation of believers done by the Lanters, though for their son, had resulted in a big testimony and peace for them. *When you intercede, you end up blessing yourself in part or even fully.*

Dr. Rob March has his own compelling story of how when his home church learned of him being at the verge of death, having been splattered by a bomb so deadly that some in the group died instantly, he credited his miraculous redemption to the tenacity of the intercession of this small country church at Shenandoah Valley. Like the New Testament church did for Peter when on death row, they went on a vigil of intercession. No way for God not to hear them. God pull him through with the effectual fervent intercession of the faithful.[46]

CHAPTER 10

LIMITATIONS TO PRAYER

The first rule of war is "Know your enemy."

Limitations are enemies of progress and fulfillment, but especially at the altar of prayer, they work to frustrate answers that are most needed. To succeed in the place of prayer, the warrior must need to identify the enemy. Prayer is like warfare. Damages must be minimized en route to victory. It is imperative that those miniature but strong maniacs must be bound, without which we struggle on our knees.

If all requests in prayer are granted the way and manner they were tendered unto God, you bet every day will look like Christmas and every night like the 4th of July. I wish that was the case, but in reality, such a picture is not real because there are candid limitations to prayers. Limitations to prayers in this chapter will be explained in forms of hindrances to prayers or factors that limit how much of or how far our prayers are answered the way we want them. Of course, we call to mind that, though, in some situations, what first appears to be unanswered prayers might turn out to be better answered at a later time, as we partly discovered in Chapter 8, "When God Answers by Not Answering." (Remember that in every circumstance whereby every prayer not answered eventually led to a favorable result, such prayers were really ipso facto answered.)

Without veering off the focus of this topic, let's just simply confirm that some good topical prayers may never be answered because of some factors. Some of these factors we must first know. Sun Tzu, handy with his theory of engaging a conflict to win, could not be handier.[47] The proposition of identifying your enemy, I term the head of the cobra that you can't spare if an encounter would end well in your favor. In the same vein identifying, that is, singling out the hindrance to our prayer, can be so key. We know its limits. Isolating what limits instigates us to be well positioned to strike the bull's eye in the closet of prayer. Thereafter, we decide how to handle them. Some of them we do better avoiding, and yet others we know and assimilate to better harness a proper and more peaceful disposition to what God is attempting to accomplish in our situations that we are committing to God in prayers.

A. SIN

The psalmist gave us a blunt reality of the clearest picture of God's take on the potency of sin as it affects the efficacy of prayer: "If I regard iniquity in my heart, the Lord will not hear me" (Psalm 66:18, KJV). This is as candid as it gets. This means simply that if I have a sin in my life that I am not willing to classify as sin or make an attempt to deal with it, such a sin is a sin by definition and fact, and whether I acknowledge it or not does not change its status before God; it will limit the power of my prayer or hinder its effectiveness or efficacy. God does not respond favorably to the prayers of sinners (John 9:31). "Who may ascend into the hill of the LORD? Or who may stand in His holy place [continues David]? He who has clean hands and a pure heart…" (Psalm 24:3–4a, NKJV) Rephrased in a simpler version—it is only those who are humbly mindful of their wretchedness and smallness before God that can obtain His attention in the place of prayers. A classic example of this thought is presented in the story told by Jesus of two men who went to the temple to pray (Luke 18:9–14). The Pharisee, who thought very highly of himself before God, though in reality, he had more issues, came boastfully before the Lord, citing every reason why God should highly regard his prayers. He was ignorant of the fact that even in the very best of our righteousness, we are still like filthy rags before God (Isaiah 64:6). But the publican, cognizant of who he really was, came humbling himself before God, expressing that he was indeed a sinner and asked for forgiveness and mercy. Aftermath: The Pharisee was condemned, and his prayers were overturned because of his haughtiness of heart, but the publican was favored. Jesus ended His story confirming that he went home justified before God.

Sin, disobedience to express provisions and demands of God, or holding contrary views to God and acting on it is very damaging to the status of prayers. Sins must be confessed before God while the heart is tailored to turn away from them. Repentance is very attractive to prayer.

When the archenemy wants to mess with someone, he seeks, amongst other methodologies, to block a man from being favored in the place of prayer. Philip Yancey rightly observes: "Satan conquers no one without his cooperation."[48] His usual tactic is to incite us to succumb to sin in our weak points. Stretching it further, he would like to get us blinded to the point where our sins blanket us, and we can no longer humbly present our needy selves before God. And yet the sin stubbornly stands between our prayer and God, who is able and very willing to answer us, except that His hands are tied where sin blocks His children off Him.

Owning our sin before God is humility that is a prerequisite before favorable disposition with God at the altar of prayer. Pope Francis' admonition would be very compatible in this regard when he says: "In prayer, it is God who must convert us, not we who must convert God."[49] A humble heart doesn't kick against the conclusion that in all realms, man ought to defer to God.

Apostle James' wise call has no equal on this plat:

"Humble yourselves in the sight of the Lord, and he shall lift you up" (James 4:10, KJV). The far end of gains at the place of prayer cannot exceed being lifted high, for that is the strongest desire of all men. But for many, sin has vowed to not let it happen. True believers cannot be restricted on matters of grace. Christ has given us a path to victory over sin that if we walk in it, sin can no longer hinder us from entering into our rest.

B. LACK OF FAITH

Without faith, we are emphatically taught; we cannot please God nor be pleasing to Him. Faith is the foundation of our relationship with God. Our faith defines us and numbers us as one of God's children. It is our status as children of God that earns us the right to be heard through proclaiming our prayers with the name of Jesus. For as many as received Him (have faith or believe in God through Jesus Christ), to them, He gave the power (authority) to become the sons (and daughters) of God, unto them who believe in His name (John 1:12). It is this power or authority vested in to our sonship that gives us an unrestricted and bold access to God.

Where there is no valid relationship, signaling the absence of faith, prayers become words and expressions without substance, which cannot be guaranteed with God. Faith that is foundational is inexistent, and so is the basis for a prayer. God is not obligated to listen to or answer the prayer of those who do not belong in His family, but on the contrary, His eyes are upon His children while His ears are opened to their prayers (1 Peter 3:12).

Illustrating the very need to keep faith alive in times of continuing prayer, Pope Francis, in a teaching on prayer, declared that it is faith that sustains prayer.[50] Citing the strings of actions that sequentially preceded the healing of Jairus' daughter, it was obvious that someone had to be loaded with faith. Having acquiesced to Jairus' petition to heal his daughter, another expeditious intervention had to be executed as they went, resulting in time being drawn out, which appeared to be a factor in the daughter running out of life. News came that she passed. But Jesus had committed to Jairus' request (Mark 5:21-33). Pope Francis observed that Jairus, for a time, had to walk in the dark with only the flame of faith. Who cares whether it was a flame or a drop or a jot or of the size of the mustard seed as expressed by Jesus (Matthew 17:20)? Bottom line: The integrity of God was at stake, and faith would be an accessory. Thank God, Jairus delivered even as Jesus always super did.

Extended to those who will savor the reward of prayer is the reminder that God wants us to believe that He can and will do whatever we truly and faithfully ask in prayer. I sincerely believe that God is plainly aware that sometimes, many are found in the place of prayer actively asking but do not believe that God will answer them. They just wanted to pray, their heart not resonating with the words. A good example can be found in the action of some of those who, locked up in a room, were praying that God would release

Peter from Herod's imposed imprisonment that was to lead to his execution (Acts chapter 12). The Lord heard the prayers and indeed answered. He was miraculously and powerfully released by an angel of the Lord, and straightforwardly, Peter went to the place where the brethren were still engrossed in intercession. When he got there, some of them were astoundingly shocked. People of faith must be resistant to shock when God answers prayer. That is what He does best for His loving people. I believe the group got away with one, perhaps, because there were some with faith who were involved. Such is the dynamism of group prayers that sometimes what may be lacking in some is supplied by the others.

Every believer must understand and believe that God is very interested in answering our prayers. You must believe and have faith in Him. Jesus strengthens us on this platform when He taught us that if a man has a faith as little as a mustard seed, one will command a mountain to move, and it sure will (Luke 17:6). This must imply that the disease of lack of faith in the place of prayer for many a believer is actually more severe than we may ever imagine. Quantifying the obvious nonsuccess in prayer on so many fronts may be indicative of this simple vice: lack of faith.

When the Lord says, "Call unto me, and I will answer thee and show thee great and mighty things, which thou knowest not" (Jeremiah 3:33, KJV), He means it. He is never a vain talker, like you and I are sometimes. Let's minimize the failure at our knees by truly believing God more when we call upon Him. When we surrender to the control of His spirit, rest assured that the Holy Spirit, who knows the mind of God and His will, always shapes our prayers to align with God's plan, whereby such prayers cannot but be heard and answered. At that level of relating, faith is in action, and manifestations of answered prayers are prolific and undeniably obvious.

C. DISCONTINUANCE OF PRAYER

Jesus teaches us to continue praying until we receive an answer. He gave us a classic lesson in this regard, citing the case of the importunate widow versus the fearless judge (Luke 18:1). The woman, helpless, needed a certain important help. Figuring that the only one in the neighborhood that could assist her was the judge, she approached him. Facing rejection a number of times, she persisted until the man decided to help her, not necessarily because he was merciful but because he concluded that if he did otherwise, the woman would continue to bug him. To stop her peskiness, he answered her. What does it matter for the poor woman as long as she receives the help she needs? Jesus summed it up: Don't give up in the place of prayer.

Pope Francis, in another segment of his earlier cited teaching on prayer, expressed that evil is the lord of the penultimate day and never the lord of the last day.[51] He described the penultimate as the moment when the night is darkest, just before the dawn. It is the in-between time following the commencement and the inner travail, but most close to the time of receiving answer from God. It would seem that for most of us who had been in a position of having to wait for divine response to prayer, it is in this "penultimate" that the devil tempts most. He must have known that these are moments or hours or days or even years that define success or failure of our endeavors in prayer. If we bungle this time, the enemy brags, but if we dig in, we emerge with triumph and songs of testimonies.

E. M. Bounds has in his credit this expression that reinvigorates the thought: "Prayer in its highest form and grandest success assumes the attitude of a wrestler with God."[52] I don't know if he was thinking about the fight between Jacob and the angel in Genesis 32:24. However, this pops out in the mind. Wherever Jacob unearthed the inspiration, he proceeded to engage this strange man in a holding up that boldly declared, "I will not let you off unless you bless me." Surely, every spirit-filled reader of scripture would agree that he was spirit led and that his action was a prayer in combat. He held tight, and the angel found himself in a tight corner. Jacob was not ready to let the angel get away under the dark. Seeing the light was about to expose his identity; he had to bless Jacob. But come to think of it: The angel was there by a divine command; it wasn't Jacob that brought him down. This fact highlights Jacob taking a timely good advantage of a divine providence in the place of prayer. The opportunity was presented, and he perseveringly took it.

Do not give up praying, especially when a special need is screaming up from your life, begging. Our God is a need supplying God. Though not all prayers may be answered spontaneously, please note that some prayers need to be offered as weapons that must gradually chip off a mountainous obstacle or problem. They may take the posture of a boxer that needs to steadily jab into submission a very strong opponent. In cases of sorts, standing strong for a season (without letting off) in the place of prayer is the only sure tactic for breaking through; and indeed, we must. Thomas Rainer's call to church leaders and pastors while stressing the need to press in prayer if the post-quarantine church in America would ultimately haul in escapades here fits. You can't just let off if nothing happens after one day of intense prayer. He charges them to teach members to pray and wait. He continues: "There will not always be immediate and apparent answers." He cited Abraham and Sarah's challenge. He further encouraged: "Be reminded from time to time of God's invisible hand at work. Don't lose emphasis. Don't stop praying."[53] Simple but solid advice!

To him and innumerable others who are thus convinced, victory is soonest at sight if we don't give up praying.

D. GOD'S RESPECT FOR FREEDOM AND SELF WILL

One aspect of human life that is very profound is the freedom we have to do whatever we want to do. The lubricant for this privilege is the ability to reason and make decisions. Bear in mind that God never forces anyone to do anything; only Satan coerces people to do what sometimes they might not want to. Through the weakness of the flesh, Satan coerces men to do things that ordinarily they may not want to do (Romans 7:7–25).

There are certain decisions you and I face that the outcome may turn God off in the place of prayer. When we really want to sin or do our own thing, God will not stop us or coerce us to desist, and when it is executed, some prayers may become a victim.

That God would not violate His own law concerning us is like a two-edged sword; good on the side of us demonstrating the high-level reasoning capacity to make sound decisions. The antithesis is that when we end up with poor choices or even flat-out wrong choices in cheer disobedience to common sense or God's law, we jeopardize good opportunities to be blessed.

God inspired us through His servant Apostle Paul: "And do not grieve the Holy Spirit of God..." (Ephesians 4:30a, NIV). Co-opting the words of Phillip Yancey, this style of imploring us shows how "the Lord of the universe could become so 'small,' so freedom-respecting as to put Himself somehow at our mercy." Words fail to capture the enormity of descent when a sovereign God takes up residence in a person and says, in effect, "Don't hurt me, and don't push me away."[54]

Many a time, in the comfort of our waywardness, we offer prayers like, "God, have Your way"; "Do whatever it takes…" Like John Donne, the poet was quoted, "Batter my heart, three-person'd God."[55] Yancey was convinced: "But God rarely does. God woos and waits."[56]

And really, therein highlighted one of the benefits of getting involved in prayer—it encourages us to deal justly and rightly with our Father God, for He is such a loving father who forever means good towards us. We must not under any circumstance allow His good nature to incite us into taking for granted the privilege of free will He had graciously granted us. Honoring this favor is to enjoy prayer fellowship with God without being hit with hindrances or even roadblocks.

E. GOD'S ENFORCEMENT OF HIS PERFECT WILL IN LIEU

Sometimes, due to the importance and magnitude of what God had planned to do, He enforces the performance of His words in accordance to His will. In the unparalleled model prayer of Jesus called the Lord's Prayer, we learn that one of the prayers of humans is that the will of the Lord will be done on earth (Matthew 6:10). Cognizant of the goodness of God and His graciousness, we know that nothing surpasses the implementation of God's will. It is for the good of all. But because man could be very inaccurate and insensible in the realm of decision-making, it has been discovered that God's enforcement of His perfect will often result in a cheer disappointment for many because His ways are rarely our ways and our thoughts, ditto…as far as the East is from the West, so are our thoughts and ways from His (Isaiah 55:8). Often, because many are superficial, what we desire in the place of prayers are contrary to what God is planning.

Therefore, in situations where God chooses to perform His will to us, it is "prayers unanswered" (but thanks to Him), though ultimately, it is a blessing because His will for us will always be better for us than our own devised plans. For instance, in *90 Minutes in Heaven* by Don Piper, having laid on one side in the hospital bed for thirteen months and swarmed by pain and hopelessness, he prayed earnestly that God would pull the plug and return him to heaven.[57] Thanks to the Lord, this particular prayer was rejected by God. If it was granted, the millions of people who later benefited from his testimony, either in print or in words of mouth, would have been robbed the golden opportunity. Most assuredly, God, in His omniscience, knew better all around. He knows when a prayer has to be particularly truncated in order that a better life might be experienced in the same situation. He came that we may have life and have it more abundantly, and we are most glad when He chooses to execute His plans even at the risk of hurting our own little personal caprices.

The prayer of a Confederate Soldier says it all:

"I asked for health, that I might do greater things;

I was given infirmity that I might do better things...

I asked for strength that I might achieve;

I was made weak that I might learn to obey.

I asked for riches that I might be happy;

I was given poverty, that I might be wise.

I asked for power, that I might have the praise of men;

I was given weakness, that I might feel the need of God

I asked for all things, that I might enjoy life;

I was given real life that I might enjoy all things.

I got nothing I asked for, but everything I had hoped for;

Almost despite myself, my unspoken prayers were answered.

I am, among all men, most richly blessed."[58]

CHAPTER 11:
GLARING OUTCOMES OF PRAYER

Prayer is like a seed that is sown; though it goes under the earth silent for a season, yet in its due season, it resurrects with unstoppable power that enables it to defy the earth that once covered it and ultimately stands taller and above. Prayer, no matter what and how long it takes, gets visibly answered.

In this chapter, we will talk about practical accomplishments of prayer in order to encourage someone that prayer did work and what it can continue to do if we do not relent. Dennis Rainer resolutely expressed the confidence he has in the effectiveness of prayer as an instrument of accomplishing a thing. He speaks about the need for prayer in the post-pandemic operation of the church universally: "But one thing we can know for certain: God honors praying churches. He answers the prayers of praying people."[59] Rainer, in essence, is postulating that the fact that you pray establishes an assurance that a response is coming from God. The only way to mute expectation is to not pray. God's answer to our prayer cannot be forever veiled. If a response is released, it will be known. Therefore, the chapter additionally will emphasize the usefulness and effectiveness of prayer as a means through which God responds to His people. Indeed, it is undoubtedly a tool that is multi-useful.

A. SEPARATING/TEARING DOWN AND PAIN

In some instances, the situations that require prayers are formed because of wrong and contaminated unions, unholy alliances, merging of noncompatible items or people, and an attempted walk by two disagreeing people, etc. Thus, part of the first major work prayer will do in such a situation is separate or tear down incompatible alliances and unions. The resultant effect of separation or tearing apart is pain. Therefore, at the initial part of combating a situation with prayer, do not panic if things appear to be breaking down and pain is being experienced. When a man is to be eternally connected with Jesus, hear what may happen in his immediate vicinity:

> *Suppose ye that I am come to give peace on earth? I tell you, Nay; but rather division: For from henceforth there shall be five in one house divided, three against two and two against three.*
>
> *The father shall be divided against the son, and the son against the father; the mother*

against the daughter, and the daughter against the mother; the mother in law against her daughter in law, and the daughter in law against her mother in law.

Luke 12:51–53 (KJV)

Meaning that very closely related people may be separated when someone seals a new relationship with God. Nothing on earth beats the gifts of salvation, but candidly, it draws a line in the sand. Sometimes, a close family is your greatest enemy, and when the Lord will avenge you, there may be separation that will cause you pain.

For instance, for Abraham to be fulfilled, he would have to go separate ways from Lot, a personal family sacrifice that wasn't as easy as it sounded (Genesis chapter 13).

The removal of the Israelites out of Egypt was a result of prayer.

And the Lord *said, I have surely seen the affliction of my people which are in Egypt, and have heard their cry by reason of their taskmasters; for I know their sorrows;*

And I am come down to deliver them out of the hand of the Egyptians, and to bring them up out of that land unto a good and a large land, unto a land flowing with milk and honey; unto the place of the Canaanites, and the Hittites, and the Amorites, and the Perizzites and the Hivites, and the Jebusites.

Exodus 3:7–8 (KJV)

But guess what? Shortly after God had visited Pharaoh with high hands, God's children had to be removed and distanced away from their Egyptian friends, familiar territory, variety of foods, and pastimes of Goshen (in Egypt). Along the way, some of their enemies were battered and decimated by the Red Sea. In that massive, unprecedented decimation, there were commotion and noise of screams of horror, reminiscent of the psalmist's words: "A thousand shall fall at thy side, and ten thousand at thy right hand; but it shall not come nigh thee. Only with thine eyes shalt thou behold and see the reward of the wicked" (Psalm 91:7–8, KJV). All these events were far from being pleasant but horror-full. They were pitiful sights, the aftermath of the initial results of prayer of deliverance coming to be answered. After which, as was the case with God's people, they would arrive at the Promised Land, God's promise eventually fulfilled.

You might say, "Well, those are their taskmasters and are getting the recompense for treating them wickedly." Okay, let's come closer home. On one occasion, while the Israelites were on their way to the Promised Land, there was a rebellion. In an attempt to purge the camp, the Lord put about 3,000 men to death (Exodus chapter 32). It is an understatement to say that for this family with a very bright, secure future, the loss of 3,000 for a good cause was a double bind. If they had their way, they'd rather make it to the land flowing with milk and honey without losing families and friends. But sometimes, that is not realistic!

Thank God that the originating prayers ultimately got answered in spite. God's people eventually arrived in the Promised Land, prophecies came to pass, and God's promise for His people eventually fulfilled.

B. BIRTHS SPIRITUAL SUCCESS AND MIRACLES

From Our Daily Bread (April 24) is extracted a write-up titled "Spurgeon's Boiler Room."[60] It continues: Five young college students were spending a Sunday in London, so they went to hear the famed C. H. Spurgeon preach. While waiting for the doors to open, the students were greeted by a man who asked, "Gentlemen, let me show you around. Would you like to see the heating plant of this church?" They were not particularly interested, for it was a hot day in July. But they didn't want to offend the stranger, so they consented. The young men were taken down a stairway, a door was quietly opened, and their guide whispered, "This is our heating plant." Surprised, the students saw 700 people bowed in prayer, seeking a blessing on the service that was soon to begin in the auditorium above. Softly closing the door, the gentleman then introduced himself. It was none other than Charles Spurgeon.

Following this thought was a word from Watchman Nee: "Our prayers lay the track down which God's power can come. Like a mighty locomotive, His power is irresistible, but it cannot reach us without rails."[61]

Simply put, no miracles will occur without prayer

in the mix. In ministries whereby the power of God will be commonly experienced or in a life that will enjoy unstoppable demonstration of God's power, prayer must be a pastime. It is amazingly encouraging that such a massive number (700) of prayer warriors were continually devoted to praying and interceding before Charles Spurgeon's services. They surely laid down the tracks through which the mighty locomotive, the practical experiencing of God's power in miracles and wonders, would be commonplace.

Jesus Christ in the New Testament era showed us the prime example. Every time He separated Himself to pray, His return had always witnessed diverse miracles and healings of all sorts (Matthew 14:23, 26:36; Luke 6:12, 9:28). Phillip Yancey refers to this Jesus' custom as spiritual recharging.[62] When energy is waning and morale is recording low, spending time in prayer is like a refill: an already paid-for that cup can be refilled without question to the cooling down of a thirsty man.

C. CREATES A FORCE

Beyond what is experienced in physical sciences, prayer creates a more powerful force in the realm of the spirit that combats the power of darkness orchestrated by Satan and his cohorts. Believers are engaged in spiritual (unseen) warfare "for we wrestle not against flesh and blood, but against principalities, against powers, against the rulers of the darkness of this world, against spiritual wickedness in high places" (Ephesians 6:12, KJV). Invariably, we are charged to be strong in the Lord and in the power of His might.

One sure way of being strong in the Lord is praying (verse 18), which resultantly creates a force that is potent with a repelling capacity to push away all the forays of the evil one. The force created in the place of prayer is second to none, attested to by the conquest capacity. E. M. Bounds says, "Prayer is the greatest of all forces because it honors God and brings Him into active aid."[63] We are urged on, "Resist the devil, and he will flee from you" (James 4:7b, KJV). The greater of our foes cannot stand his ground in the place of prayer, for "the effectual fervent prayer of a righteous man availeth much" (James 5:16b, KJV). Prayer is powerful and works wonders. I, therefore, charge you to create a no-touch family, home, environment, community, etc., for yourself by engaging in prayer.

D. CREATES A BATTLEGROUND

In the place of prayer, a battlefield is created where life's critical battles are won. The enemies that lurk around seeking us to kill, steal, and destroy, we lure into these battlefields that they cannot resist to their own ruin. Herein, our Father God, the Mighty Man of War, shows up with His unmatched power. We are further pepped up by J. H. Jowett:

> We must conquer all our circumstances in the battlefield of prayer. We must, first of all,

> *bring them there. We must survey them there.*
> *We must master them there. In prayer, we*
> *bring our spiritual enemies into the presence*
> *of God and fight them there. Have you tried*
> *that? Or have you been satisfied to meet*
> *and fight your foes in the open spaces of the*
> *world?"*[64]

In this form of battleground, not only are exterior enemies drawn to be demolished, even the enemies within (of the mind) can be dealt with in the place of prayer. The psalmist testified: "I sought the LORD, and he heard me, and delivered me from all of my fears" (Psalm 34:4, KJV). This is kind of hilarious! The enemy sometimes uses our minds against us and is so confident because of the proximity that he would surely secure a victory against us. But thanks to our God for giving us prayer as a tool to combat the foes in the most unlikely places, practically catching them unawares.

The battle of the mind is very fierce. The Lord encourages us to be forewarned, "For God hath not given us the spirit of fear; but of power, and of love, and of a sound mind" (2 Timothy 1:7, KJV). Prayer can be very effective at safeguarding our hearts and minds because from whence oozes out the issues of life (Psalm 27:14, Proverbs 4:23). We cannot surrender them to become an enemy within. That would be a house divided against itself.

Don Piper spoke proudly of what prayer helped him to achieve with regards to the battle of the mind that he was drawn into following his gruesome accident that sent him to heaven for ninety minutes. Sunken deep in depression, he wished for death. Unable to turn his side for over one year was a catalyst to clinical frustration of immeasurable order. But God turned deaf to his wishes, and God's people continued to pray, and eventually, from his mind, he began to perceive life and survival that today he could enjoy with all glory yielded to God.[65]

Not refuting that for some, and in some instances, prayers could be a delight; however, generally, in the "battlefield," according to Allen, prayer could be travail. In those times, prayer is like meeting the enemy face-to-face on the battleground. We have to fight for what God says is rightly ours, dragging it by force from our adversary, the devil.[66] No doubt, this invokes the aura of Warfare 101. There are times when we must wrestle in prayer, like Jacob, when he cried, "I will not let thee go, except thou bless me" (Genesis 32:26b, KJV). There are times when the answer is slow in coming, and we must hold on patiently like Daniel, who waited three full weeks (Daniel 10:2). Yet some other times, this wrestling may leave the body weary and the nerves overwrought, as in the case of Elijah when he prayed down the fire and rain (1 King 18–19:4). We must press because the battle will not outlast us, for we are more than conquerors through Christ who loves us (Romans 8:37). In the place of prayer, we cannot lose the battle if we do not faint. And faint we will not in Jesus' name!

E. PRAYER WORKS

Since the creation of man, prayer has been working and effective. While Jesus was on earth, He prayed severally and obtained innumerable answers in very profound manners. He taught believers to pray and how. Today the power of prayer has not dwindled. As a matter of fact, the more compelling the need for you to pray, the more astounding the dimensions of answers and approval.

It is amazing to see how what appears to initially look like a minor prayer result led to a staggering effect. Peter's release led to the growth of the church (Acts chapter 12). Just imagine if the church had not gathered together to intercede for the apostle, a non-move that would have erased any chance of divine intervention, meaning that he would have been killed. And had he been killed, maybe the church would have been driven into extinction! The fact that the church convened to pray and the entire New Testament church took off after that rescue had muted the contra conception. No doubt, prayer works!

Science is not mute on this point. We have found, as revealed by results of medical researchers from leading hospitals and universities across the United States, that belief in God is really good for you, making you healthier and happier and helping you live longer. "Studies have shown prayer can prevent people from getting sick, and when they do get sick, prayer can help them get better faster," Duke University's Harold G. Koenig, MD, tells Newsmax Health.

He further expressed that an exhaustive analysis of more than 1,500 reputable medical studies indicates that people who are more religious and pray more have better mental and physical health. And out of 125 studies that looked at the link between health and regular worship, eighty-five showed regular churchgoers live longer. "There's a lot of evidence out there," wrote Dr. Koenig, director of Duke's Center for Spirituality, Theology, and Health and the author of several authoritative books on faith and healing. He declared that a striking study published in the *Southern Medical Journal* demonstrated that prayer has a remarkable effect on patients with hearing and visual deficiencies.

After prayer sessions, they showed significant improvements based on audio and visual tests. He added:

> *The benefits of devout religious practice, particularly involvement in a faith community and religious commitment, are that people cope better. In general, they cope with stress better, they experience greater well-being because they have more hope, they're more optimistic, they experience less depression, less anxiety, and they commit suicide less often. They have stronger immune systems, lower blood pressure, and probably better cardiovascular functioning.*[67]

For the devoted and the steadfast, there has never been any doubt that prayer has the power to make situations better. So, I charge you to pray, pray, and pray. Do not relent. Prayer is a seed that is sown; remember, for as long as there will be life, seed time and harvest will not cease (Genesis 8:22). Your prayer will be answered if only you pray.

Because I have been taught to pray from childhood, over the course of my life, I have experienced my Father God in uncountable dimensions and shades of answered prayers. God has answered specific prayers; He has answered general ones. He had granted me high-profile gadgets, and He has, on the other side, given me simple things specifically asked for. I remember when I was ten, I asked God for a specific Christmas wear, and He used my pastor to provide it. God has amazed me in small and big things, low and high platforms, and the common denominator being: He is a prayer answering God for all who trust in Him and ask in faith.

In the entire ordeal that Don Piper experienced, he summed up by saying: "Perhaps the greater miracle is that people prayed and God honored their prayers." "No matter how delayed."[68] Hyatt Moore was unflinching and resolute, "Prayer gets answered."[69] And so convinced, Don Piper put himself on record: "I believe part of the reason I am still alive, as I've already pointed out, is that people prayed. Dick Onerecker prayed me back to life—to live without brain damage. David Gentiles and others prayed so that God wouldn't take me back to heaven just yet." In a yet more reflective tone, he continued: "I am here, I am alive, and it's because God's purposes have not yet (all) been fulfilled in my life. When God is finished with me, I'll return to the place I yearn to be. I have made my final reservation for heaven, and I'm going back some day—permanently." He wraps it: "Prayerfully, I'll see you there too."[70]

It seems to me that many of us who have found our niche in the undeniable power of prayer could not be otherwise convinced!

Therefore, I charge you: don't leave money on the table. Pray. Call upon the Lord. Sow the seeds of asking Him. Surely, He will reward you with an answer, and you will have testimonies; for nothing can overcome you.

EPILOGUE

Our world of today is enveloped with clouds of troubles, diseases, wars, discords, challenges, and lack. Many people are not doing well. But the scariest part of the story is the many who do not know the Lord and some believers who may be retracting farther away from eternity with God. All these, with many more that the luxury of this book cannot accommodate, have a shot to experience reversal if we can start entreating God in prayer. It's a beginning step and action that can neither be faulted nor regretted. To not consider doing this is tragic. I can't agree any more with F. B. Meyer when he expressed with concern: "The greatest tragedy in life is not unanswered prayer but unoffered prayer."[71] Prayer can practically make everything better. More so, prayers are effectively prayed, which guarantees great responses from the Lord.

But prayer cannot pray itself. You and I will have to pray to squeeze out of prayer its inherent sweet juice. We are the ones that have been instructed to pray without ceasing. It is a call that puts us into a position of honor to be partners with God in His quest to get great things done in the lives of people and our world.

If on that alone, I commend us all to give praying a shot at tackling any issue we are confronted with. That is, the way it has been eternally scripted that you are victorious through Christ Jesus, who, by way of His unparalleled love, died for you and secured you a prayer stamp in His name that will forever guarantee a reply to your bidding.

If you have never obtained eternal life through faith in the Lord Jesus Christ, which implies that you are not guaranteed an answer when you pray, I encourage you to ask Jesus Christ to save you and become your Lord. The answer to this prime prayer is a surety if you want it. With that granted, you become a child of God with a prayer-answering privilege when you pray in the name of Jesus, who just saved you. Congratulations!

ABOUT THE AUTHOR

Dr. Ayodeji Awe is the founder of Our Savior's Church, a nondenominational church in Houston, Texas. With the assistance of his wife, Debra, he has been the senior pastor for twenty-seven years. He attended universities in Nigeria and the United States, obtaining his doctorate in theology at the International Seminary, Plymouth, Florida. He is an erudite theologian and a board-certified chaplain.

He started his writing ministry in 1976 as a coordinator of the Youth Association in Christ Apostolic Church in Nigeria. He is a published author, poet, and composer of gospel songs and hymns. Some of his books include: *Perhaps! God will change His Mind*, *Men in Transit*, *Now that You Are a New Creation*, and *Why Do the Heathen Rage?* He's been referred to as a man with a giant pen. He is a religion columnist with *The Houston Punch*, *Christian Trumpet*, and *Christian Herald*, where he answers biblical and Christian life questions sent in from all works of life. He is the publisher of the *"Running Eyes" Newspaper*, a publication that shares with the whole world the good news of Jesus in various facets.

An anointed speaker, Dr. Awe's voice is well respected in churches and the community. He was the public relations officer for the Nigerian Christian Association in Houston and is a member of the Board of Trustees of Greater

Houston Ministers Fellowship.

With Debra, his wife, they are blessed with four adult children—Tolu, Jumoke, Damilola, and Olakunle, all musically talented and supportive in ministry.

ENDNOTES

INTRODUCTION

1 Rainer, S. Thom, *The Post-Quarantine Church: Six Urgent Challenges and Opportunities that Will Determine the Future of Your Congregation* (Illinois, Carol Stream: Tyndale House Publishers, 2020), 55.

CHAPTER 1
What Is Prayer?

2 Ehiemua, Victor, "Prayer as a Lifestyle." Article written for Christian Herald: September 2020.

3 Singh, Sundar, "Thoughts on Prayers Compilation" (TPC) by Yemi Ayodele (missioncares@aol.com/ February 18, 2012), 1.

4 Murray, Andrew, TPC by Yemi Ayodele. Ibid., 4.

5 Jowett, J. H., TPC by Yemi Ayodele. Ibid., 4.

CHAPTER 2
Essentiality of Prayer

6 Luther, Martin, TPC by Yemi Ayodele. Ibid., 1.

7 Ehiemua, Victor, Ibid., 20.

8 Boom, Corrie ten, TPC by Yemi Ayodele. Ibid., 2.

9 Bunyan, John, TPC by Yemi Ayodele. Ibid., 2.

10 Payson, Edward, TPC by Yemi Ayodele. Ibid., 2.

11 Bounds, E. M., TPC by Yemi Ayodele. Ibid., 3.

12 CAC Praise, Worship and Revival Songs. (Akure: CAC Supreme Council, 2010), 100.

13 Yancey, Philip, *Prayer: Does It Make Any Difference?* (Grand Rapids: Zondervan, 2006), 123.

14 Teather, David, "Bill Gates gets 4m a day"/ Technology (New York, guardian.com, November 19, 2004).

15 Oke, Wale Bishop, Preaching at Chapel of Restoration, Houston, 2007.

16 Luther, Martin, TPC by Yemi Ayodele. Ibid., 1.

CHAPTER 3
Facilitators of Prayer

17 Chambers, Oswald, TPC by Yemi Ayodele. Ibid., 2.

18 Erondu, Felix, "Handle with Prayers" (self-publishing, 2013), 33.

19 Oyakhilome, Chris, "Rhapsody of Realities" (June 13, 2013), 34–35.

20 Hinn, Benny, *Good Morning, Holy Spirit* (Nashville: Thomas Nelson Publishers, 1990), 103.

21 Bassey, Nathaniel, Album "Holy Spirit Carry Me," 2020.

22 Malgo, Wim, *Called to Pray: How to be a Prayer Warrior* (W. Columbia: Midnight Call/Olive Press, 1996), 55.

CHAPTER 4

Prayer as a Tool

23 Erondu, Felix. Ibid., 4.

24 CAC Supreme Council. CAC Hymnal (Brooklyn, NY, CAC. Supreme Council, 2010), 686.

25 Newsmax Health. "Science Proves the Healing Power of Prayer" (Newsmax.com, March 31, 2015).

26 He was the founder and first general evangelist of CAC.

CHAPTER 5

Forms of Prayer

27 Yancy, Philip. Ibid., 125.

28 Dickens, Charles, *Martin Chuzzlewit* (New York: Knopf, 1907), 145.

29 Yancey, Philip. Ibid., 125.

30 CAC, Praise, Worship, and Revival Songs (Akure: CAC Supreme Council, 2010), 151.

CHAPTER 6

Peculiarities of Prayer

31 Bunyan, John. Ibid., 2.

32 Bounds, E. M. Ibid., 3.

33 Malgo, Wim. Ibid., 67.

CHAPTER 7
Power Ingredients of Prayer

34 PUSH—"Push Until Something Happens." (Gives a connotation of aggressive posture in the place of prayer, like Jacob did. Press on until God answers.)

35 Booth, Mary Warburton. Ibid., 3.

36 Yancey, Philip. Ibid., 100.

37 Yancey, Philip. Ibid., 100.

38 Murray, Andrew. Ibid., 3.

39 Allen, A. A., *The Price of God's Miracle Working Power* (Bottom of the Hill Publishing, 2012), 75.

40 Allen, A. A. Ibid., 75.

41 Piper, Don, *90 Minutes in Heaven* (Grand Rapids, MI: Revell, 2004), 42.

CHAPTER 8
When God Answers by Not Answering

42 Yancy, Philip. Ibid., 198.

43 Piper, Don. Ibid., 72.

CHAPTER 9
Intercession

44 Malgo, Wim. Ibid., 54.

45 Holton, Chuck, *The Photo That Answered a Prayer* (Oregon: Multinomah Publishers, 2003), 166.

46 Holton, Chuck, *The Grateful Warrior*. Ibid., 168.

Chapter 10

Limitations to Prayers

47 Sun Tzu, *The Art of War* (Shambhala, 2005).

48 Yancey, Philip. Ibid., 84.

49 Pope Francis/Carol Glatz, Weekly Address, San Damaso Courtyard of the Apostolic Palace (Catholic News Service), May 30, 2021.

50 Pope Francis, Weekly Sermon, Wednesday Audience-Feast of St. Philip Neri: "Why does it seem like God doesn't answer our Prayer sometimes?" May 26, 2021.

51 Pope Francis. Ibid.

52 Yancey, Philip. Ibid., 100.

53 Rainer, Thom. Ibid., 64.

54 Yancey, Philip. Ibid., 85.

55 Donne, John. *Sermons on the Psalms and Gospels*, Evelyn Simpson Editor (Los Angeles: University of California Press, 1963), 226.

56 Yancey, Philip. Ibid., 85.

57 Piper, Don. Ibid., 72.

58 Holton, Chuck. Ibid., 188.

CHAPTER 11

Glaring Outcomes of Prayer

59 Rainer, Thom. Ibid., 66.

60 Daily Bread. "Spurgeon's Boiler Room" (April 24, 2014), 2.

61 Nee, Watchman. Ibid., 2.

62 Yancey, Philip. Ibid., 79.

63 Bounds, E. M. Ibid., 2.

64 Jowett, J. H. Ibid., 2.

65 Piper, Don. Ibid.

66 Allen, A. A. Ibid.

67 Newsmax Health. Ibid.

68 Piper Don. Ibid

69 Moore, Hyatt. Ibid.

70 Piper, Don. Ibid. 205.

EPILOGUE

71 Yancey, Philip. Ibid., 283.